"Eugene Acevedo's book is a handy tool for anyone seeking to climb the ladder in the corporate world to read and to keep in his library. Sharing the insights he gleaned while going from a degree in physics to the CEO of the Rizal Commercial Banking Corporation, he discusses the elements that leadership in business entails."

Cesar and Joy Virata
Former Philippine Prime Minister, and
Former Artistic Director, Repertory Philippines

"This is not just a book. It's a masterclass, shaping leadership with soul, a smile, and smart strategy. Eugene blends wisdom and wit to move you from good to great, from capable to compelling. This isn't 'shelf-help.' It's mindset fuel. Read it, reflect deeply, lead boldly, and live with purpose. Bravo, Eugene!"

Francis J. Kong
President of Success Options Inc.

"Eugene Acevedo's *The Future Leader* is a unique blend of management insight, experience, and thought-provoking commentary. With clarity and heart, he charts a roadmap for a visionary leadership in a digital world. A game-changer for anyone looking to level up their leadership skills and seeking relevance, resilience, and real impact in emerging markets."

Jaime B. Aristotle Alip, PhD
Founder and Chairman Emeritus at CARD MRI

"Only someone who began as a physics teacher, became a transformative CEO, and returned to school at 60 to pursue a DBA could write a book like this. *The Future Leader* distills Eugene's insights on AI-first reinvention, leadership practice, and personal journey into a guide that is both intellectually rigorous and deeply human. It's that rare kind of book—analytical without being cold, ambitious without losing its soul. For anyone navigating disruption or guiding others through it, this book is both a map and a mentor."

Bernadette G. Bernabe
Founder and CEO, MME Connections | Multimedia Exponents

THE FUTURE LEADER

**What It Takes to be
The Next-Gen CEO**

Published by

World Scientific Publishing Co. Pte. Ltd.
5 Toh Tuck Link, Singapore 596224
USA office: 27 Warren Street, Suite 401-402, Hackensack, NJ 07601 *UK office:* 57 Shelton Street, Covent Garden, London WC2H 9HE

Library of Congress Control Number: 2025025171

British Library Cataloguing-in-Publication Data
A catalogue record for this book is available from the British Library.

THE FUTURE LEADER
What It Takes to be The Next-Gen CEO

ISBN 978-981-98-1645-3 (hardcover)
ISBN 978-981-98-1762-7 (paperback)
ISBN 978-981-98-1646-0 (ebook for institutions)
ISBN 978-981-98-1647-7 (ebook for individuals)

For any available supplementary material, please visit
https://www.worldscientific.com/worldscibooks/10.1142/14401#t=suppl

Desk Editor: Geysilla Jean Ortiz
Cover Design: Jimmy Low

Project Managed and Typeset by Manila Typesetting Company (MTC)

THE FUTURE LEADER

What It Takes to be
The Next-Gen CEO

Eugene S. Acevedo

Rizal Commercial Banking Corporation,
Philippines

World Scientific

NEW JERSEY · LONDON · SINGAPORE · BEIJING · SHANGHAI · TAIPEI · CHENNAI

About the Author

Eugene S. Acevedo is the President and CEO of RCBC, one of the largest banks in the Philippines, and a multi-awarded leader in digital banking and business management.

Eugene is a former university physics instructor. He completed his MBA at the Asian Institute of Management (AIM) at the top of his class and as a J. Nepomuceno scholar, and entered Citibank as an executive trainee. In 23 years, he had assignments across Asia, the last being as Managing Director and Head of Global Markets for the Hong Kong and Taiwan Cluster. He was previously Head of Asia Derivatives Structuring and Sales based in Singapore. In addition to his business management roles, he sponsored management training programs and chaired the Markets Asia Recruitment Committee. He left Citi to serve as President and CEO of the Philippine National Bank.

Eugene started his leadership journey by chairing his La Salle high school student council. At the University of San Carlos in Cebu City, he later on led five student organizations. He was a consistent scholar; he majored in physics, which he finished with *magna cum laude* honors. He received the National Science and Technology Award for Academic Excellence. For further studies, he took the Advanced Management Program at Harvard Business School. At present, he is taking his doctoral studies at AIM.

Eugene has published two books, *Never Stand Alone* and *Reinvent and Outperform: Becoming a Better Leader*, which became Fully Booked bestsellers. He posts regularly on LinkedIn, and has been recognized as one of the Top 10 and Top 30 Leaders for LinkedIn Philippines. In April 2025, Eugene's *Never Stand Alone* received the Gold Quill Award for Writing, presented by the International Association of Business Communicators (IABC).

For Francis,

with love from Dad

Indebted to

Chairperson Mrs. Helen Yuchengco Dee

for the honor of leading RCBC

Table of Contents

Prologue: More Than Words

I write because, for whatever biological reasons, I now tend to forget easily. I write because I find some thoughts entertaining. I write so I do not lose those thoughts and will get the chance to share them.

Ideas can fly out as quickly as they fly in. I can't even point out exactly what prompted them. But appear they do, and they are welcome.

I have also begun to realize that I have a distinct manner of writing. I tend to alliterate, using successive words where the first letters sound the same. Sometimes, I deliberately exaggerate to emphasize. I am enamored with English-style rhetoric, but I practice it more when speaking and less when writing. I cannot control how the words are read, even if I wish they were savored rather than rushed. Perhaps I should record myself reading? Maybe not.

I also like contrasting. Why? Because I find that things and ideas are best described as they are and as they are not. It also spices up the statement with a bit of drama. You might notice that my default sentence tends to have a clause, then a comma followed by a "but." It is like a pendulum that swings, making the readers figuratively pivot their heads.

Then there's the occasional joke, but hidden within a play of words. I must admit those give me much satisfaction.

Words move, words persuade, words lift. Even if, in the end, I am the only one reading the fruits of my labor, it will be more than enough. For words will move me.

Introduction

With Much Gratitude

I started to compile this book on December 31, 2024, in Bukhara and Samarkand, Uzbekistan, two of the main stops on the Silk Road, and centers of ancient empires.

The previous month was way more than I expected, and I owe my friends, collaborators, and colleagues for how it went well. I got my biggest surprise walking into the Fully Booked store in BGC seeing *Reinvent and Outperform* placed on the bestsellers shelves, ranking number 4. After the book launch early in the month, I brought my team with me to Singapore for the second book launch at the Book Bar, organized by my publisher, World Scientific, and hosted by Eric Sim. I was overwhelmed to see my former colleagues from the Asia regional treasury team of Citibank; it became a reunion.

I am grateful to LinkedIn for the platform that has allowed me to reach 670,000 individuals and generate 6.7 million views in the last 12 months when I started becoming active. I am thankful to the PT30 organization for naming me Top Corporate Leader and one of the Philippines Top 30 Leaders on LinkedIn for 2024, and to New In Asia for the distinction of being one of the Ten LinkedIn Top Voices to Follow in the Philippines.

Never Too Late

I have discovered new passions late in life, and they have sustained my enthusiasm for more action and challenge. Who said being 60 meant slowing down?

I never knew I was going to enjoy writing this much. I write at least 3 hours a week on LinkedIn and this is my third book. I started out as a reader, accumulating over a thousand books over time. Now, I have distributed or sold more books than I have ever read. I expected to run out of steam 6 months ago, but I have kept going, putting my thoughts on new topics and fields of interest.

Seven years ago, I started going on a learning overdrive, obtaining ten certifications over a 6-month period to prepare for my current CEO role. That thirst has never been fully quenched. Now, I am back in graduate school almost 40 years later, pursuing a doctorate in business administration. Saturdays are now fully allocated to statistics and data science, and studying society's grand challenges of climate change, plastic pollution, social inequality, food security, and many more. I thought that I would have less time to write; I actually ended up with more topics to write about.

I have always had strong convictions about the ability of education to solve social inequality and promote social mobility. That is why time spent on school boards is worth every minute. It is an obligation and a repayment for the educational opportunities my three schools provided me. I started as a teacher and might be one again in the future.

Mentoring is the only way I know we can truly turn talented young graduates into outstanding bankers. I must have mentored almost 200 previously. This year, I formally took on another 40, with another 20 calling themselves my virtual mentees as they follow my posts and send me notes regularly. This has inspired me to write about career development, leadership, strategy, and similar issues that junior and middle management professionals face daily in the workplace.

For someone written off as "can't speak" in high school, I now spend hours on stage every month. Internal opening or closing remarks are standard, same with town halls. The real thrill comes from external keynote addresses on various topics related to my work. Where do I get my material? From my two books and my LinkedIn posts, of course.

All these form a Venn diagram with many intersections. Or, in a regression, five variables with significant multicollinearity. Doing all of them requires the equivalent effort of two uncorrelated hobbies.

Is there anything else? Yes. I am still frustrated about not having musical skills. I did the sax for a short while, but the guitar has still evaded my grasp. Maybe in my wildest dreams, I really want to be, God forbid, a rock star.

Part One

Building
Leadership Skills

JOAQUIN "JACK" C. RODRIGUEZ, SR.
District Governor

"

I have to keep
looking and
not wait for the
apple to fall.

Chapter One

The Race is On

Does one really plan on being a CEO? Apparently, yes. For me, what triggered my ambition was reading about young leaders from humble backgrounds successfully climbing the corporate ladder. If they can do it, maybe I have a chance as well.

Somehow, stars have to align to give me an edge. Breaks may not be available. I have to keep looking and not wait for the apple to fall. Stars align when talent meets the right resources. Such was the case for Renaissance artists. For chess grandmasters. And for champions.

My proof of concept was a gentleman who I later met when I was already a senior banker at Citibank; he was an acquaintance and remains one. I, in turn, have become proof to younger colleagues that the top job is a real possibility.

But Why Next-Gen CEO?

I recently stumbled upon an article about what keeps Jamie Dimon awake at night. It got me thinking about how the business landscape has changed over the past 15 years. Back in 2010, when I first stepped into the CEO role, life was already pretty complicated. Fast forward to today, and the complexities have multiplied. Here's my take on the evolution of CEO worries.

One of the most significant shifts has been the move from internal to external issues. Fifteen years ago, we were primarily inward-looking, focused on internal operations, employee satisfaction, and similar issues. Now, we're constantly keeping tabs on global and regional conflicts that can wreak havoc on interest rates and foreign exchange.

Welcome to the age of cybersecurity nightmares. Today, CEOs are haunted by the thought of bad actors getting more sophisticated with "Day Zero" malware and local scam artists preying on our customers. Gone are the days when our biggest tech worry was a crashed computer and unsaved files.

Who could have predicted that pandemics would become a regular topic of conversation? The COVID-19 pandemic was a wake-up call, reminding us that we need to be ready for the next viral problem that visits our shores. Fifteen years ago, "going viral" was figurative, referring to social media. Now, it is something we fear literally.

The global value chain is more interconnected than ever. When disruptions occur, they affect everything from products sold in Manila to the flow of raw materials. Remember when supply chain issues meant your package from overseas was delayed? Now, it means condominium developers are facing rising costs due to limited steel supplies.

New digital businesses are making traditional business models obsolete at a scary pace. Every day seems to bring a new app or platform that's ready to revolutionize the industry. Adapt or get left behind has never been truer. CEOs must constantly keep learning while unlearning outdated practices. It's a delicate dance of staying current and agile.

Moreover, the role of a CEO has evolved dramatically over the past 15 years. From global conflicts to threats, and the rapid pace of technological change, the challenges are numerous and complex. But with the right strategies and a forward-thinking mindset, we can navigate these turbulent waters and lead our organizations to success.

In conclusion, fostering a culture of innovation and resilience within the company is crucial to staying ahead of the curve. Building strong relationships with stakeholders and maintaining transparency can also help in managing uncertainties. Ultimately, the ability to adapt and embrace change will define the success of next-generation CEOs.

Not Entitled to Anything

Real life does not give participation medals. You might get Latin honors in college for studying hard, but you don't necessarily land a good job. It might increase your chances, but not if you insist on a degree that has little commercial value.

When I majored in physics in the 80s, everyone wondered aloud what I was going to do after university. (My answer: banker, after my MBA.) My *magna cum laude* honors did not result in any job offers, except from the faculty.

Just because I studied hard did not automatically mean I got rewarded. My skills had to be relevant. Then, there might be others who had better resumés than mine. Thankfully, because of the demand for data scientists, physicists are now attractive recruits.

If you aspire to be a CEO, you compete with thousands of others in the company. I can tell you that, for starters, you need to be an expert in at least three disciplines, and revenue-generation, i.e., sales, better be one of them.

What if I became an entrepreneur instead? Just because I took a risk to build a new business does not mean I will be profitable. Just because my business is trying to solve society's wicked problems does not mean investors will come with baskets of funding. Just because I have the purest of intentions does not mean customers will line up outside my store. I have to earn the right to their money.

Whatever I am selling has to solve a real (not just imagined) customer problem better than other products available in the marketplace, at a competitive price, with convenient service. I have to compete with everyone else. Fortunately, over time, setbacks gave me new learnings that increased my chances of success.

It is always good to remind ourselves that the world does not owe us anything.

An "A" for Effort

When I was a young banker, coming to the Citi trading room early, reading the news about the markets while savoring two pieces of choco butternut donuts, and not leaving in the evening until I finish my tasks were just part of the job. This was simply how we grew up.

My colleagues and I carried these habits as we moved to new roles and employers. Even as we automated, this just meant we became more productive, but our work ethic remained unchanged.

This is why I am bothered when I hear about hard work being underestimated, even ridiculed. Is it the way people are raised, or perhaps the safety net of opportunities that makes them take their careers less seriously? Why is diligence seen as a sign of weakness? What's so terrible about being early for work? And for putting in extra hours because you are committed and you enjoy what you're doing. The same is true with work from home (WFH) and flexi-time, where some employees start at different times but still put in their fair share.

For many young employees, hard work is their only ticket, their path to bettering themselves and their families. Of course, work should avoid invading personal time when you need to rest and recharge. If it does, it should do so infrequently. There is no need to be purists; technology has thankfully made it easier to balance work and personal lives anyway.

Effort is a big deal. Effort gets noticed. Effort inspires. And most importantly, effort turns failures into resilient success. Think about that persistent salesperson who never gave up and eventually won your admiration through sheer diligence.

Let's talk about working smart. I actually do not see any problem with this. When paired with hard work, it is a powerful combination that leads to even greater results. Work hard, and smart!

Hard work is the unsung hero of success. It builds character in ways that shortcuts and instant gratification never will. It may not give you an "A," but you stand a better chance of getting one.

The Motivation Mechanism

I just read an article by Deci and Ryan (2000) entitled *Self-Determination Theory and the Facilitation of Intrinsic Motivation, Social Development, and Well-Being* from the American Psychologist. It delves deeply into employee motivation, focusing on basic psychological needs for competence, autonomy, and relatedness. The theory gained traction in the mid-80s around the time I was completing my MBA, which explains why I never heard about it before.

But it does not sound new to me because it seems like common sense. If you believe that you are doing well at work, if your supervisor gives you enough latitude in how to accomplish your task (and does not breathe down your neck), and if you have a support system and belong to a "tribe," you will be motivated to come to work every day (or do WFH).

As leaders, we have to recognize that we need to satisfy the component needs in order to motivate our teams. Above this, I have also tried to understand what drives each of the leaders under me. Their self-determination can be fueled by ambition, the sheer joy of learning, being competitive, and giving their family a comfortable life, among others. Whatever their reason for performing, competence, autonomy, and relatedness are minimum requirements. If employees do not get this in our organization, they may look for it elsewhere.

The good thing about intrinsic motivation is that work itself is its own reward. It reduces or diminishes the dependence on financial incentives.

I was also curious about how motivation affects the business, and cautious about self-reported performance, hence I looked for evidence in a sales organization where performance tends to be more objective. In a 2017 study *Motivational Factors in Sales Team Management and Their Influence on Individual Performance* by Ferreira, Ramos and Marques (2017) on over 300 pharmaceutical salespeople, she found that "personal goals" and "skills acquired" were the most significant intrinsic motivators, consistent with the SDT theory. She also found that there was a strong correlation between motivation and business results.

I've seen firsthand how highly motivated salespeople consistently achieve higher sales targets and demonstrate greater customer satisfaction. This correlation really drives home the importance of fostering intrinsic motivation within our teams to ensure business success. By investing in the personal and professional growth of our employees, we can enhance overall performance and achieve sustainable growth. It's a powerful reminder that when we support our team's ambitions and development, we all thrive together.

Old Enough to be CEO?

In the last decade, I often read articles about CEO age, and off the top of my head, I recall those suggesting that early to mid-50s was ideal—a good balance between energy and experience.

I remember I was 45 when I first took the top job at PNB. Frankly, I could have used more wisdom at that time, but the job called for transformation. Such strategy required physical and mental stamina. You must be a bit of a spring chicken as major strategic moves demand substantial face time with employees, clients, and the industry.

Transformational posts are not nine-to-five office jobs. If you want to grow faster than your peers, you have to be in the field, putting in long hours.

Curious about what research says about this, I found a peer-reviewed article titled *Managerial Ability, CEO Age and the Moderating Effect of Firm Characteristics* by Desir et al. (2023), published in the Journal of Business Finance & Accounting. The paper suggests that the ideal age of the CEO depends on the type of company. Innovative companies like start-ups and technology firms need younger leaders who have the energy and ambition, and whose cognitive abilities are still sharp. On the other hand, highly regulated and more stable companies require leaders with more experience and a deeper understanding of the complex regulatory framework.

Which brings me to my question—what if you are in a company that is radically transforming, but part of a highly regulated industry? The CEO needs to be an energetic, sharp senior citizen, someone who is battle-tested, goes to the gym three times a week, and spends hours studying.

I will end this by saying that we should start thinking of the senior leadership team as the company's leader. This way, we can provide the company with the right mix of skills, ambition, experience, energy, gender, backgrounds, and even patience.

Have You Sold Anything? Managed P&L?

When we were in sixth grade, we sold sandwiches and ice candy to raise funds. I don't remember what for. What I recall was that our "durian-flavored" coconut ice candy was a huge hit.

That may have been my first innovation, but it was quite accidental. You see, someone happened to have stored durian in the small freezer of our GE refrigerator together with our ice candy pieces. When I took my goods out the next morning to place in an ice box, it smelled of durian. We offered it as coconut ice candy, but the durian smell was so overpowering that it sold quickly.

That project taught me selling early in my life which was, unfortunately, not sustained. The next time I went cold-calling was when I was 28, selling derivatives solutions and foreign exchange hedges. Presenting our products, persuading customers, and closing deals continued my hands-on training.

Selling is a mandatory skill. Now, I strongly recommend that young people volunteer for sales roles early. Not knowing how to sell is career-limiting.

P&L means profit and loss. Managing P&L means you have run a real business or division, had to meet sales targets, persuaded customers, closed deals, supervised performers, controlled costs, and so on. It implies a multitude of experiences and skills.

To many business executives, running a P&L proves character and whatever else that is difficult to list down. Basically, that you lay parts of your body on the line, and are prepared to be accountable. You are beyond theoretical, you are battle-scarred. You quote less from a book; your lessons are from real life.

There still are leaders who move up in the business world without the pressure to directly produce results. The higher they go, the greater the stakes. They may never be given the chance for the top jobs.

Winning the CEO Job

I had coffee with one of my mentees last month, and our topic was how he should prepare for a CEO job.

He had already heard of my "triple threat" speech before, and that was the first thing we needed to discuss. Has he built expertise in three disciplines? After they take important roles in support functions, I always urge my mentees to volunteer for a sales job, where they demonstrate the ability to generate business. Whether they like it or not, revenue generation skills and the ability to manage a P&L are mandatory. You don't get that certain level of respect from your peers and subordinates until you make money for the company.

Some executives take a shortcut. They jump directly into sales leadership roles without doing one-on-one selling. That kind of works if they are able to build customer relationships and inspire sales teams. But there is something cinematic about winning stripes in the field that makes a CEO more relatable.

The minimum requirement is a record of consistent leadership performance. That puts you on the short list.

But first, you need to win the job. Never assume that your current record will stand and will be sufficient. Why—because the CEO position is a different job. I am convinced I won my three CEO opportunities because of one single reason: communicating a compelling transformation strategy.

When I succeeded, it was because I did my homework and could recite my transformation and growth plan over an hour or two. I convinced the decision-makers that I knew what had to be done, that I had done something similar before, and that I could hit the ground sprinting. The interviewers obviously want to get to know you, but they need a credible, inspiring plan. The journey of preparation is itself enriching.

Making it to Managing Director

Among bankers who work in global institutions, achieving the Managing Director (MD) position is considered the pinnacle of success. However, it also comes with its challenges. During job cuts, MDs are often the first to go.

Every year, groups of MDs gather to discuss and justify nominations for new MDs. Names are supported and challenged. Does the candidate belong to our peer group? Another division can block the appointment even if the candidate's supervisor is strongly endorsing. This process ensures that only the most deserving candidates rise to this esteemed position.

There is a ritual behind this. After the announcements are made, the names of new MDs are posted in the Wall Street Journal, and each newly minted MD receives an acrylic plaque with the names of their cohort. I still have my plaque in my office. This tradition symbolizes entry into a distinguished group of leaders.

My turn happened in 2005. At that time, I had just moved back to the Philippines as country treasurer after relinquishing my role as regional head for derivatives structuring and sales. I was hopeful that I would be promoted because my previous assignment carried significant profile and financials, but I couldn't be certain until I was called to the country CEO's office and heard the news.

To be honest, I was floating on air that day. It was not only a great feeling of personal achievement but also a profound sense of relief.

Finally, becoming an MD was a reminder to start planning the next phase of my career. MDs tend to have a tighter time decay, meaning the pressure to perform and stay relevant is ever-present. Achieving the MD title may evidence the skill and the ability to navigate the complexities of the banking world, but to me, it was a reminder to pursue my second career dream.

Just Got Lucky

When people ask for advice or when I read about others giving guidance, I always hesitate because a nagging question lingers in my mind: "What if I/they just got lucky? What if I was actually wrong?"

To paraphrase Shakespeare (1601): "Some are born lucky, some achieve luck, and some have luck thrust upon them." (I replaced the word great and greatness with lucky and luck, respectively.)

I don't envy people born into privileged families; they have their own, possibly bigger, share of demands. They may have the inside track with their elite preparation and network of connections, but it comes with significant pressure to perform like their parents, right from childhood.

When young people ask me how to become a CEO, I share my thoughts and give my "work hard" spiel. I mention my biggest sources of good fortune—my mentors. They have taken great care of me and found opportunities for me. I had to be worthy, of course, or they wouldn't have chosen to mentor me. As they say, the teacher appears when the student is ready.

I also mention that being available at the right time is crucial. I can prepare and over-prepare, but there may not always be an opening.

I often say it's not that I don't believe in luck; I just believe more in preparation. And preparation includes studying the subject matter at hand.

When joining industry panels discussing digital transformation steps, I can tell a whole story. Recently, I decided to finally study this matter once and for all. I cannot just keep pointing to probabilities. There must be a formula to follow to ensure we have a higher chance of success.

Ultimately, I recognize the role luck has played in my journey, but I lean heavily on preparation as the secret of my success. Luck, as they say, is just preparation meeting opportunity. Here's to being ready when the breaks come your way.

Trigger Happy

My work environment as a junior trader put a premium on quick absorption of information before 8:30 AM, and being ready for the market when it opened. As I moved up the ladder, I demanded the same discipline from those who had the "misfortune" of being under me. Decisions had to be quick as opportunities could disappear as soon as they showed up; speed had premium.

One of my colleagues often repeated the phrase, "hesitation kills," although I found that to be an exaggeration. Nonetheless, it underscored the competitive nature of our work.

When my team approached me for advice or a decision, I responded quickly. I would ask for a bit more detail to complete the story, but that did not take long. Much of this had to do with knowing the terrain, the internal rules and banking regulations, and the confidence built over time. I could not be *"teka, teka,"* Tagalog for "wait, wait." This quick decision-making often showed up in my 360-degree assessments.

I had a senior colleague who would be ready with a five-sentence explanation, and I would entertain myself by saying yes after the second sentence. What she did not understand was that I already trusted her to make her own calls. My "yes" was an affirmation of her seniority, although I found it delightful to give an answer before she finished her treatise.

Knowing the boundaries and having the ability to solve customer problems quickly and creatively within those boundaries is a skill I looked for in young people. We had a middle office that ensured we stayed within our limits, but I preferred self-restraint first and controls second. I was convinced that this approach fostered a sense of responsibility.

I realized soon after that I needed to explain my decisions later. Part of the apprenticeship nature of the trading room was instinctive mentoring. We clarified our decisions during breaks or lunches.

What I did not do during the actual live situations was ask, "What do you think we should do?" I only did that when structuring derivatives deals, as we had the luxury of time, and I saw the benefit of brainstorming.

As I moved out of the trading room and into broader managerial roles, I realized I needed to change. When discussing a credit approval, for example, or a change in strategy, I asked for inputs and gave people time to clarify their points. I appreciated the value of diverse perspectives.

At first, I did not do it for morale reasons. It was simply an intellectual exercise to elevate the best ideas. The collaborative environment that followed was something I learned to treasure.

Did I evolve because I got older, because of new roles, or because I was working with teams that had different working styles? My professors would say, each factor added a coefficient to the regression line, explaining 90% of the variability.

What stayed consistent was the sense of urgency.

Corporate Pedigree

Pedigree comes in many forms. One is family background, or social standing. Second is education, particularly the best schools in the country, or premier graduate schools here and abroad.

In the corporate world, you get branded for having worked long in the accepted best training grounds, especially if you started from the junior ranks in those companies.

In marketing, there is always a premium given to P&G and Unilever officers. Both companies are considered the best places to learn brand management from. Chief marketing officers tend to be sourced from them. If tech, the IBMers rule. They have a way of dressing up, of walking into a room. Many of them lead various tech companies as country CEOs.

In banking, Citi occupied this prestigious spot for decades. It was dubbed the graduate school of banking, a 'UniverCiti'. In most countries around Asia, CEOs of half of the country's big banks are Citibank alumni.

Being a Citibanker is treated like a badge of quality. Recruiters are aware of how intensive and international the training programs are, and the manner by which bankers are exposed to stretch and foreign assignments. This is particularly true when the banker started via the management associate or analyst program.

Hiring a Citibanker (IBMer, P&G, or Unilever alumni) is like a shortcut; you assume there is a high probability that the person comes with the right skills and attitude. For good measure, you can always get confirmation from their alumni network.

I spent 23 years there, starting as an executive trainee. Working with HR, I mentored dozens of exceptionally bright young bankers. Not all of them made it through the program, although the success rate was high. Those who did well, and are now Managing Directors in various financial institutions, had the right attitude to match their skill sets.

Job, Company, or Manager, Which to Choose First?

Start with job or career. Find something you enjoy or, better yet, love doing. Make sure it has great career prospects and will enable you to meet your financial needs. And be honest with your competencies, while building skills required to advance.

Company next. Culture is crucial. Do they help build your career? Are they customer-focused, collaborative, and innovative? Are they one of the leaders in the industry? Avoid toxic companies. Ask around, you will always find someone who knows someone else. Do your research.

Finally, your manager, when possible. Choosing your boss is ideal, but often not possible unless you come in at a mid-career level. Oftentimes, you are assigned to work under a manager when you come to the office for your first day.

One way to evaluate an organization is to check its willingness to put leaders in positions where they need to start from zero in terms of skills required for the job. For example, I once assigned a cash management senior to run the corporate bank. Then I moved a marketing executive to lead a regional salesforce. Citi once moved me to the North Asia regional audit team, and later to HK to be a derivatives structurer. Why do companies do that?

First, faith in the person's soft skills, and that he/she will learn the rest of the required hard skills in quick fashion. Oftentimes, the new competencies enhance the person's profile. Second, it builds the next line of succession. Future leaders have to be experts in several products and functions. They get tested in business cycles doing different roles. Third, network. Moving people around judiciously builds stronger camaraderie around the company.

Finally, when your company takes a risk on your career development, you need to do your best to deliver.

What Matters More is the New Company, Not the New Job

When receiving offers for a new job, it is understandable that pay, title, and position will drive the excitement. They appeal to the ego. High positions put you ahead of your peers. Fancy titles affirm all the hard work that you have put in.

But that would only be half, even a third of the consideration. You need to fit into your new home. Culture match is what will give you peace of mind, peer collaboration, and senior guidance. Without this, you will not look forward to going to the office. In fact, you will want to be out the door soonest.

I have heard a few sad stories from mentees, and read letters of those I mentor "virtually." Of course, I check if they had invested in building relationships in the first place. But if the new company is toxic, no amount of goodwill will help.

Before I joined RCBC, I did my homework. I found out as much as I could about the owners, the leaders of the bank, their activities, what they stood for, and more. I was convinced RCBC was the right place for me to spend my final years as a banker. Now, it is my role to convince younger leaders to join our management team and banking family.

It might be too much to ask, but do you love your workplace? I do.

When Your Job Does Not Excite You

Not everyone gets lucky ending up with a job they really enjoy and derive fulfillment from. Sometimes, what you thought was THE job for you turns out to be a dud. What do you do?

First, maybe you over-expected and needed to scale down career advancement expectations. Consider this job as a stepping stone toward the one that you really want. Play the long game. Be patient.

Second, keep learning. Build your resume so that you increase your chances of getting closer to your ideal job. Get certified. There are plenty of free courses available. Volunteer for tasks.

Third, invest in your network in the office. Do not wait for everyone else to adjust to you. Having friends makes the environment more tolerable.

I greatly enjoy what I do now. But, even if this was the career I chose, there were times in my previous assignments when I did not feel I was in the right place. In fact, my very first post right after the management training program felt like I was shortchanged. It was unexciting compared to what previous batches got. Just the same, I was learning to become a better banker, and had a lot of friends.

Decades later, I am convinced that my first assignment in the back office actually made a significant difference in how I supervised teams, how I transformed operations, and made me a more complete banker.

"

You cannot demand from your team something that you cannot model yourself.

Chapter Two

People are Complicated

When I was a junior, I just did my thing as best as I could, and trusted that my boss would take good care of me. This worked 83% of the time. I hardly nagged for a promotion, salary increase, or training. One conversation was all it took, if needed.

As a senior, I enjoyed taking care of my younger colleagues. There were just a few that took more time than usual. They asked for meetings to discuss their salary, were more obsessed about their promotion, or were concerned that their peers are doing better in other companies. They consumed a lot of my energy.

Half in jest, I told them that the door was wide open.

Tom Brady on Leadership

I am not a fan of the greatest athlete to play American football (I follow John Elway and the Denver Broncos), but I happened to read a really insightful article by Brady one early morning. Somehow, since social media algorithms know I follow his co-author (Nitin Nohria, former HBS dean), Brady's leadership principles showed up on my Facebook feed.

My three takeaways are team goals precede individual glory; work harder than other teams and set higher personal and team standards; and care about each teammate deeply but know how to motivate each one.

Teamwork is most difficult to build when there are stars who put their individual performance goals ahead of the team's. This is worse when this leads to blame and mistrust. In the end, it comes down to attitude. You can only do so much coaching. Bad attitude is bad attitude. If the person has decided for himself that he does not belong, find a more suitable replacement.

As I have written before, there is a premium to preparation and hard work. But what really makes the difference is showing the team they can raise their standards. If the target now is X, how can we make it 1.5X? I have learned that training, tools, and incentives can result in better performance.

The leader's work ethic is crucial; he must model the behavior he wants to encourage. Work the talk.

Finally, the article was a good reminder that people have different motivations. Getting to know them well—including their backgrounds and personal circumstances—allows the leader to understand the right triggers. Interestingly, you will also find a bold few who just outperform no matter what.

When you find a crew of motivated, highly skilled performers who collaborate and put the team's goals ahead of their personal interests, then you have a better chance of winning. Like I sometimes say, I manage my senior leadership team as a championship sports team.

Hire Smarter People

We always hear the phrase "hire people smarter than you" or "if you are the smartest person in the room, you are in the wrong room!" What do these actually mean? Let me try to give my views.

People should be smarter than most others in their specific field of expertise. For example, my digital banking head is one of the leading experts in the country; he even chairs the industry organization. I have the same recruitment objective for every single leadership function under me. This way, my colleagues and I will learn from each other, and pull each other up.

It is much like a sports team where there are specialists who play their roles well and add value to their teammates.

Over my more than 30 years as a banker, I have built skills in treasury, in consumer finance, retail banking, corporate banking, and a number of other functions. I have strong familiarity with the control functions having helped establish those roles in previous banks. I have also made a significant effort to learn data science and digital skills. But since I don't focus on those jobs full-time, I expect my lieutenants to take intellectual leadership in their specific fields. They are smarter in their specific roles.

I admit I have this habit of "parachuting" into groups to go micro on projects every now and then. It keeps me updated without needing bureaucratic reports. I also get to learn from mid-level officers, and I make mental notes on the ones who made a good impression. When the topic discussed happens to be something I have substantial experience at, I make sure I contribute, or challenge certain points, as it adds to the learning process.

Finally, having smart guys around is useless if they are not generous with their knowledge or if the people they are with do not have the intellectual humility to listen and understand. In fact, if you don't share, or if you don't listen because you insist that you are the smartest guy in the room, we are better off with you leaving.

Listening Rewires Brains and Relationships

In high school, my classmates were those I grew up with, so I listened to understand. I was in a safe environment with my close friends. In college, there were recitations and discussions, while debates mainly happened in organized sessions in minor subjects. I must confess, I relished those encounters with liberal arts majors. Otherwise, there was little to debate about in physics, which was my major.

When I was in grad school in the 80's, listening in class meant being ready to pounce or defend. Quite literally, my ears were on my toes. Our professors would pick on anyone to start or continue a discussion. The class felt like an informal debating club. This was particularly stressful for me early on as I had no business background and couldn't hide behind the phrase "based on my experience." My only job before my master's was teaching physics.

When I entered the job market, my brain was already wired differently. I spent most of my time in global markets, which was not exactly a relaxed job. When I switched to the sales side, I noticed a gradual shift in my behavior, as I paid more attention to the customer, not the markets.

A sales job, if done right, can indeed change the way you think, talk, and listen. In sales, you listen to understand, not to argue. This is exactly why I press my mentees to volunteer for sales roles.

There is more. I also discovered that the act of repeating what the other person said made me understand them better. The act of confirming helps, not just to acknowledge politely, but also to be more thoughtful. The science behind this involves our working memory, allowing us to focus and ignore distractions while connecting new information with knowledge stored in our long-term memory.

In the end, the ability to listen deeply rewires not just our brains but our relationships as well.

When a New Employee Underperforms

In any organization, hiring officers and supervisors have the obligation to find the right employees, train them to increase chance of success, and continually assess if they meet the standards. If new employees don't make the grade, it is best to admit that the person's skills may be a mismatch for the job. If it is an attitude or reliability problem, identify it early and avoid making it a burden for the rest of the team.

After interviews, the next step is to provide adequate training to ensure the person succeeds in his/her new role. (Many jobs do not need further training, especially mid-career ones.) That early, trainers can evaluate the new employee further. Is he/she able to learn new skills, does he/she have the necessary aptitude? Does the trainee come on time, and relate well with other employees?

The company has many opportunities to identify red flags early before the 6-month probationary period is over, for example, a frequently tardy trainee, one that has trouble staying awake in class, or flunking the exams. These employees need to be immediately warned and removed if they don't comply with second chances they have been given. Don't wait for the 6-month period to be over.

Based on experience, attitude/reliability issues are extremely difficult to fix. Don't waste your time giving many chances.

The 6-month probationary period is like a "6-month interview," where the supervisor can continue to assess performance. I think this is similar in many jurisdictions.

As always, make sure HR is involved in the process. Even within the prescribed period, some employees may still decide to sue you. Best to get everything documented so you can demonstrate fairness. HR will also have to be convinced that the supervisor is not at fault.

How Do You Build Trust in the Workplace?

A consultant asked our team one weekend, and my instinct was to say "plant trust to harvest trust." It has to start with people learning to work together, by trusting each other with simple tasks, which leads to bigger tasks, even if they find out later that there are some they don't want to work with. It does not take long for anyone to distinguish between those who are trustworthy from those who are not.

If you use Google Scholar to learn about trust, there are even a number of proposed psychological frameworks. I did not come across any of them in the past and, therefore never used them. Instead, I simplify trust into competence and reliability. Can the person do that task assigned? Will he/she do it?

Forgive my very basic construct, but this comes from my being a banker. When lending, we assess the capacity to pay and willingness to do so. The two are not the same. During normal times, there may be no concern or reason to doubt. But during periods of difficulty, this is when you see the difference.

As a first-time supervisor in the late 80s, I quickly sized up the competencies of my team members. I knew who the experts were in which areas. I was also aware of tardiness, absences, and similar reliability concerns.

The first solution was to train two back-ups for each unique task. That minimized reliability as an issue. But one particular task bothered me. It had to do with advanced treasury accounting for which only one clerk had the skill to accomplish. I couldn't be vulnerable to possible reliability issues, so I learned how to do it myself. Some say "trust but verify." I prefer to trust but have a plan B.

Finally, trust is a two-way street. You cannot demand from your team something that you cannot model yourself.

Trust vs. Competence: A Quantitative Perspective

I have read books and listened to authors talk about how trust is more important than performance or competence, and how leaders should start their interactions by building a solid base of trust. Simon Sinek (2020) brilliantly described the perfect Navy SEALs example on YouTube, highlighting how low trust is toxic, and that lesson has stuck in my head. I often repeat it in the bank, as sustaining a top-performing organization is at the core of my priorities.

Lately, I've been pondering on the trust-versus-competence discussion once more. Naturally, it is best to have both, and you can indeed find leaders with both attributes. It is understandable that CEOs recruit those they know from previous assignments, as these leaders have been battle-tested. New hires are vetted by asking their former colleagues about their performance as teammates.

While laboring through statistical problem sets, an idea came to me. This is how I frame it:

Trust should not be measured on a 0 to 100 scale. Trust is more like correlation; it is measured from negative one to positive one, or from negative 100% to positive 100%. Competence, on the other hand, may be viewed the traditional academic way. If recruitment is done right, it is realistically somewhere between 70 and 100, as the person has sufficient domain expertise. A mid-performer can be, say, an 85. Trust at the lowest part of the scale means not trustworthy at all and can be negative one (or negative 100%). The two are measured very, very differently, and our choice of words fails to grasp the significant quantitative difference.

When I trust someone, we don't have to be fully correlated, but we need to have much in common. (In physics, mistrust is like a vector with a strong magnitude but pointing toward the opposite direction.)

I might be over-explaining this, but at least, to me, I think I have finally understood why. And I found my answer in the most unlikely place—a dispassionate one at that.

Loyalty and Friendship

I finally met Irza, my Singaporean mentee, who I have been in touch with for several months now. He is a brilliant, multicultural young man, and with admirable personal advocacies. One topic we discussed at length was loyalty, and the reality of colleagues leaving for other opportunities. He experienced this in his company. I faced this at Citibank where at least half of our high-potentials were poached consistently.

I shared that I have learned to accept that hard reality. I can empathize with the person, and his/her financial and career needs. At the least, he/she now becomes part of my personal network. I choose to focus on taking care of those who decided to stay, and to make it worth their while.

This brings me to a related topic on loyalty awards. I finally got an award after 10 years at Citi where I spent a total of 23 years. My next tours of duty were 7 years and less. Was I loyal? I'm sure I was. Quantity does not count unless there is quality. Loyalty demands that you care for the organization and contribute to its success.

When I started as a Citibanker, I worked long hours until we figured out ways to make processing more efficient. I happened to be assigned to the "salt mines" where leaving late was the norm. Everywhere I went afterward, I applied myself with similar dedication, which only started to diminish when I made the decision to move out.

Beyond providing exemplary service, you look for ways the organization can improve. There will be times when you need to go above and beyond the call of duty, and you do it willingly. You advocate for the company's products and promote it as a great place to build a career. You show this on social media. If you work in a bank, you use the bank's credit cards. You defend the company's reputation when it is criticized.

When you are loyal, you are "all in!"

What Makes Good Advice

Should I take advice from people who haven't done my job or have never been responsible for similar financial results? The answer is: it depends.

I obviously prefer to listen to industry veterans whenever they are available. This comes from experience in banking, where I grew up being mentored by some of the very best at Citi. Then I had the benefit of working with industry veterans in retail banking, consumer finance, and other parts of the bank.

Their firsthand experience and war stories can provide invaluable and entertaining insights. They've been tested through several economic cycles and a number of crises. Their varied types of experience offer a level of breadth and depth that is hard to replicate. What they cost me is time. And all it requires is active listening.

However, it's also important to consider younger experts who specialize in new, innovative fields. They bring fresh perspectives on the latest trends and technologies that can be valuable in our rapidly evolving industry.

One key factor in assessing the value of advice is the advisor's track record. This can be tricky to determine, as victory has many fathers. Many companies, collaborators, and consultants claim credit for successes. I recall sitting in presentations where, in a single week, two sets of consultants name-dropped the same client as their success story.

To be frank, I believe I can identify the good advisers, the ones with brilliant ideas. They usually have industry veterans in their ranks. Listening to them can feel like drinking from a firehose of knowledge. However, I often realize that my team is already capable of implementing those that I heard. There were exceptions when we paid for services.

In the end, it's about finding the balance between leveraging external expertise and trusting my team's capabilities.

Expensive Hires: The Physics of Hiring

One morning, I had a short chat with one of my group heads who complained that external hires are expensive and distort the pay scale. His arguments were valid, but I wanted to dive deeper into the root of the issue. I asked him about the roles he was hiring for and the resumes he considered. My response was straightforward: hiring for experience will naturally be expensive.

Think about it through the Laws of Motion. Experienced professionals, who are comfortable and progressing in their current roles, are like objects already in motion. They will not change direction (i.e., move to our bank) unless acted upon by an external force. In this case, that external force is an attractive offer that compensates for their comfort and career stability. This means higher salaries and incentives, which can indeed distort the pay scale.

This brings us to two more sustainable approaches:

Hiring High-Potential Talent: Highly motivated juniors are self-propelled. They are eager to learn, adapt, and grow. Investing in these individuals can be more cost-effective and can help build a robust pipeline of future leaders. This is where management training programs are key.

Promoting from Within: Hiring externally should be complemented by a focus on cultivating talent from within. Investing in the development of internal juniors fosters a culture of continuous learning and improvement within the organization. It rewards the performance-driven kind of loyalty. This approach not only prepares future leaders but also enhances overall employee satisfaction and retention.

When you find a self-propelled and experienced recruit, that is even better. It's about striking the right balance between leveraging the experience of established professionals and harnessing the potential of emerging talent.

The New Hire Is Paid More

This is an issue that often sparks employee complaints: "I am loyal but I am paid less. It is unfair. "First of all, how do they know the salary of the new employee? Well, people talk. Assume a theoretical population where bankers at manager rank across all banks are paid around the same rate. What will it take for Bank A to poach Manager X from Bank B? Let's simplify. For starters, Bank A will have to pay a higher salary for the following reasons:

A. It will be foolish for X to move to Bank A, a totally new environment with a new set of people, without a premium to compensate his/her for uncertainty and discomfort.

B. X will lose tenure when he/she moves, and will receive a lower retirement multiple from the new bank. He/She must be compensated through a higher monthly salary.

C. Bank A will pay for new business (like new customers) that X promises to bring. Or new ideas and products. Naturally, his/her new supervisors will not forget to collect on these promises.

D. At least in theory, the new bank saves on training cost as X is already a veteran.

E. X may be hired as part of Bank A's succession plan because the current bench is not strong enough.

Obviously, X needs to deliver. If X turns out to be a star, the complaints will gradually dissipate. If the reverse happens, management will have to take action or make adjustments.

Just the same, it is crucial that pay across ranks and functions be benchmarked against the market on a regular basis. Top 10th and 25th percentile performers should be paid a premium; otherwise, they risk being poached. There needs to be differentiation, or the good ones become the next Manager X.

Performance and Performance

Performance is a basic requirement at work, but what about performance during company parties?

My curiosity led me to Googling the topic. What I saw were anti-comments, many of which were bordering on insurrection. It was generally described as a violation of rights when attendance to company parties was compulsory. They should be optional, I read. Understood.

What about the practice of making new employees sing and/or dance during Christmas parties? I did that. I sang even when it was not the holiday season. (Please make me sing!)

Is it truly a violation of rights? The employee can surely refuse, and there won't be any official repercussions. I have yet to see this happen, though. Somehow, maybe if there is enough food and beer, even the shy ones muster enough courage. And they post it on Facebook the next day as a rite of passage.

Social acceptance is midway in our hierarchy of needs. Certain rituals are part of this process. Like getting coffee for senior traders or offering to take lunch orders. In an industry that is professional while apprenticeship-based, certain traditions continue to be observed.

You, obviously, can say no. When you do that, don't expect to be treated like you are part of the tribe. Don't expect the veterans to grant you any special favors.

Angry Customers

A couple of years ago, a customer came to one of our branches and treated the branch manager rudely. She even sent me a note complaining about her experience.

Luckily, I knew the branch manager quite well. She was an earnest, polite young woman from a humble background and a solid performer. Still, I checked what exactly happened (we have CCTVs), and discovered that our staff treated the customer as best they could, but she was unreasonable and unjustifiably rude.

This happens, though not as frequently as you might fear. There are customers who exhibit bad behavior without any valid reason. I don't believe it's entirely due to the "customer is king" mantra; more often than not, it's a personality issue. Fortunately, these customers are very rare.

Occasionally, customers become angry when we make mistakes. We do our best to appease them. Criticisms anyway are also one of the best ways to improve and innovate. During these instances, while we need to make sure we empathize and solve their problem, I am also conscious of my obligation to support and protect our employees. They shouldn't endure abuse just to keep a customer.

Banking is more than mere transactions; it is about relationships. What rude customers fail to realize is that companies (not just banks) can refuse service to undesirable patrons, especially when our employee's psychological safety is on the line.

Most customers treat us with respect and kindness. In these relationships, it's no surprise that my colleagues go the extra mile. It's simply human nature to reciprocate goodwill. Mutual respect fosters mutually beneficial relationships. Those who miss this point lose out on the many benefits such relationships bring.

"

Networking isn't just about who you know; it's about who you continue to know and grow with.

Chapter Three

Pain is Inevitable

One of my few favorite reminders is from Haruki Murakami, that there will always be discomfort, but whether you suffer is up to you (Murakami, 2008). The author, being a runner, knows what he is writing about. Once pain sets in, it is indeed up to the runner.

This applies to the workplace as well. Pain comes in many forms: toxic environment, stressful targets, backstabbing colleagues, to name a few. Naturally, it is best if these negative things do not exist, but that is not realistic. They are present in varying degrees.

I am often asked for advice. I tend to get reminded of Frank Underwood's two types of pain. There is pain that makes you stronger, that builds character like pain from the gym and from hard work. But there is also useless pain, like toxic environments. The latter is a waste.

When I Was Not Good Enough

In 1985, I entered the Asian Institute of Management as a Javier Nepomuceno Scholar. I had nil business experience, though I had at least 4 years as a student leader. My college major was physics, so I had zero business subjects as well. The average age of my cohort was 25.5 years. I just turned 21 and was the youngest.

I had to study double time to erase my handicap and build some advantage, but I had financial issues as well. That was fixed when I took a part-time job to pay for the dorm and my daily expenses. (It was a full-time program.)

My grades were happily tracking an honors average, and I topped the Dean's list a number of times. In my second year, I realized I needed funds for my thesis. As luck would have it, a Taiwanese businessman needed someone to write a feasibility study for a wooden door factory, and he was willing to pay 10,000 pesos, a generous sum at that time. So, I took that second part-time gig as well.

Unfortunately, even if I ended with the highest GPA enough to graduate with honors, my thesis missed the distinction cutoff by the slimmest of margins. I knew my thesis topic was underwhelming, but this was on me, and the faculty had their own reasons for not overriding the deficit.

Over three decades later, I found myself back on campus as an Executive-in-Residence, an honorary faculty position. I enjoyed giving talks and participating in school activities. Then, I was elected to the Board and now serve as Vice Chair. Five months ago, I joined the first DBA class.

I credit the school for preparing me for my banking career. Citibank wouldn't have hired me into the Executive Training Program if not for AIM. That set me up for senior banking roles later.

I also credit the school for telling my younger self that I was not good enough.

Making My Losses Count; Bouncing Forward

Over breakfast, my wife asked me about the kindergarten incident when, not knowing English, I was unable to follow the teacher's instruction to put my brown bag down next to my desk. I was still holding it close to my chest as if my life depended on it. The whole class, and the parents watching by the windows, all saw her come over and gently take my bag.

How was I affected by the incident? I still remember it vividly, so there might have been long-term effects. The thing is, I remember a string of similarly embarrassing events throughout my schooling, almost every year had one incident that stood out. They just hit me even if I was not attempting anything extraordinary. It did evolve, however, as from grade six onward my mistakes happened when I started exploring life beyond the comfort of my books.

One thing was always clear, though: I usually bounced forward. Not content with just making the grade, I had to outperform the past, to beat my old self.

This trait carried on. In AIM, my marketing professor deliberately embarrassed me in class to make an example. He did it for show. He gave me very high marks later and had a cordial chat with me, but only after I had a massive loss of confidence that thankfully lasted only a couple of days. I did well in his class to recover from the loss of face. To be fair, I still quote him in the office, so maybe I learned a thing or two.

Last year, I felt I let the bank down when we lost the top award from a national organization. I gave my best during the final presentation, only to be told afterward that the rankings were already decided before the presentations. Should I have just read my script instead and just made do with a sufficiently decent effort? Nah. Win or lose, the show must go on.

Lose with style. And bounce back. There is no glory in losing without trying.

When You Leave Your Current Employer

I wrote about this when I saw a stray message from a close former colleague as I was transiting in Dubai.

Leaving a company doesn't mean you sever ties with everyone there. In fact, maintaining friendships with your mentors, colleagues, customers and those you had great working relationships with is a smart move.

You continue comparing notes, sharing opportunities, and swapping industry trends long after your last day. The Spice Girls (2007) nailed it when they sang about friendships not ending. Sure, your official email address may change, but your Viber number and LinkedIn messages don't have to. You stay in touch through Viber chat groups. (The Citibank Philippines alumni group has over two thousand participants!)

Networks built from former companies are a treasure. Think of it as an exclusive club where the membership perks include insider tips, industry secret, and job referrals. You still share those "Remember that time…" moments, now with the added flavor of your new experiences. And let's be honest, it's much more fun to succeed together. You can rely on those who know you to protect you, even if you're no longer sharing the same office space.

And as for your detractors? Good riddance! There's no better feeling than leaving behind the office politics, false news publishers and naysayers. Picture this: you're out there, thriving in your new role, while the memory of those who tried to drag you down fades into the background. That's a cause for celebration if there ever was one.

Staying connected with your former colleagues and mentors can lead to unexpected collaborations and opportunities. It's like a never-ending episode of "Friends," minus the Central Perk coffee. So, keep those professional bonds strong. After all, your career journey is better with good friends by your side and a fewer detractors in the rearview mirror.

Networking isn't just about who you know; it's about who you continue to know and grow with.

Dealing with Bad Bosses

Honestly, I hesitated to include this topic, but I did it anyway because this seems to be a legitimate problem in the workplace.

It is puzzling why unqualified people sometimes manage to move up the ladder and become bosses. There are several reasons for this. First, they might have been exceptional individual performers, leading to their promotion into management roles without the necessary soft skills. Second, they may have ascended due to their ability to navigate office politics. Or third, their seniors are blind.

I've had a few bad bosses in the early part of my career around Asia, and here's how I dealt with them:

Case 1: The Universal A**hole—In many cases, bad bosses are universally disliked, making them a thorn in everyone's side. If you're dealing with such a person, the best strategy is to keep away and let the natural course of office politics play out. Often, their behavior will eventually get them fired.

Case 2: The Upward Manager—A more challenging scenario involves a bad boss who is adept at charming higher-ups while being rude to those below. In this situation, you and your team need to address the issue by talking to HR. Initially, HR will try to coach the boss to improve their behavior, and will inform the seniors.

Case 3: The Powerful Insider—The most difficult scenario is dealing with a bad boss who holds significant power within the organization. Documenting specific incidents of misconduct and presenting them to HR can help build a case. While it may take persistence, HR can take steps to address the issue, even if the person holds considerable influence within the company.

In summary, while dealing with bad bosses can be incredibly challenging, there are strategies to navigate these situations. Whether it's stepping aside, involving HR, or collectively addressing the issue, it's essential to take action and not suffer in silence.

Dealing with Harsh Critics

One of my mentees spoke to me one time to ask for advice on office politics. Here's what came out of our conversation.

Understandably, harsh critics can lead to low morale and a diminished sense of self-worth, but succumbing to this would mean giving up and letting your critics win.

The best way to manage harsh critics, especially those unredeemable backstabbers, is by winning despite their efforts to undermine and undercut you. Excel in your work, outperform them, and look your best while doing it. Let your success speak louder than their whispers. Maintain a positive attitude, focus on your goals, and ignore their negativity.

Surround yourself with supportive colleagues and build strong alliances. Most likely, you are not the only victim. Anyway, misery loves company, although I admonished my mentee from being miserable.

By staying professional and unbothered, you show them that their tactics are futile. Remember, your success is the ultimate response. Keep racing, and let them eat your dust.

But wait, the critic might have a point. Constructive criticism can be valuable. Separate the useful feedback from the noise and work on that weak point to improve your performance. Critics remind me of designated persons who followed victorious Roman generals as they paraded in the main streets. Their task was to carry the laurels and keep uttering the words "memento mori," which meant "remember you are mortal," to keep the generals grounded.

Navigating office politics isn't always easy, but it is part of the territory. With a clear head and a strategic approach, you can rise above the noise and let your achievements speak for you. Remember, your success, professionalism, and resilience will ultimately prove your worth.

Detractors You Meet on the Way Up

One of my mentees—an upwardly mobile senior executive—asked me about dealing with detractors in one of our sessions. It was on his list of questions he sought guidance on, and it bothered him to some extent.

A quick background: in some cultures, or if raised in a provincial background like I was, we initially try to keep the peace. We were not raised here and we have few friends. My instinct at the start was to avoid confrontation and seek acceptance, leading us to try to please others. However, we must not overdo this as it can become dysfunctional and hinder good business practices.

As you move up the ladder, you certainly need allies. You win them through personal interactions or collaborating on projects, thereby gaining mutual trust. But you cannot please everyone, especially if you are promoted to posts that others coveted.

I assured him that detractors are part of the territory. As he moves up, encountering detractors is inevitable. In fact, some insist you haven't achieved much or stood for anything worthwhile if you don't have any critics.

I also cautioned him to pay attention to criticism, as they might be legitimate and offer room for improvement. Critics who mean well can become your best allies if you take their feedback constructively. There are times when it will be difficult to discern.

I inquired if he had senior supporters and mentors at work, and indeed he had. Thankfully, they outnumber the detractors, and they can provide him with air cover.

Finally, I urged him to try building professional relationships with the naysayers. They may not be fans of his, but give them no reason to hate him. As one of my mentors once advised, during difficult interactions, be firm but be respectful. Or, put another way, disagree but don't be disagreeable.

The Non-believers

Over time, I have realized that there will always be a group of non-believers, or those who have strong opinions, also suspicions, that will be difficult to address. And then there are those who make all sorts of excuses.

What do you do? Here are some tips:

1. There are ways to help people convince themselves to buy in. I once learned the SPIN method (Rackham, 1988), where it was more effective for people to think for themselves. Facilitate by describing the situation and the problems being faced. Imagine the implications to us if we do not do anything and get left behind. It is best when they explicitly state what needs to be done.

2. Have a target or goal that inspires, that connects emotionally. Dislodging a competitor, for example, appeals to the competitive ones, especially when we keep tracking our pursuit.

3. Create excitement with early wins. When we started our digital transformation program, there were many fence-sitters. When we won our first major award, the digital banking team started to gain hundreds, later thousands, of supporters.

4. You may have to micromanage objections. One time, when leading a sales team, one salesperson gave me excuses for why her customers were not yet converted. I decided to join customer calls and then fixed each problem.

5. Move ahead even without their support. I remember this clerk who thought he had leverage over me. What I did was master his function and once did his work when he was on a long break. When he came back, I told him that his work could be done in a much shorter period of time; he was no longer indispensable.

There is a flip side to this. When facing change, there will be a group of immediate adapters who are supportive and don't need much convincing. Treasure them.

I've found that these individuals can become your champions, driving the change forward and positively influencing others. Their enthusiasm and willingness to embrace new ideas can create a ripple effect throughout the organization. By recognizing and rewarding their efforts, you build a strong foundation for successful transformation and foster a culture of continuous improvement. It's amazing how their support can make all the difference in navigating change.

When I Thought the Boss Was Wrong

To be clear, these were situations when I mistakenly thought that the boss was making a wrong decision.

When I was a younger banker, I clarified his decision by giving him a few crucial facts that he might have missed, and depending on the situation, proposed alternatives.

If he was firm, I tried out his proposed plan first and made it work. After all, since he was more experienced than I was, there was a greater chance that he was right and I was wrong.

If you are a Star Wars fan, you could recall many instances the master and the apprentice disagreed. In fact, you can say that those movies consist of a series of master–apprentice disagreements.

If his plan did not work despite my earnest effort, I went back to the boss and suggested an alternative course of action. Majority of managers prefer that we try out their idea first before we outright disagree with it. There are a minority of bosses who are open to constructive debate.

The reality is, the boss and the subordinate do not have the same level of knowledge, of experience, and of contextual understanding. There is asymmetry. But it is also in this asymmetry where the transfer of knowledge and skills happens.

There was an instance when I worked under a senior who always insisted he was right even if his decisions were obviously bad. I did not bother thinking about leaving; he was on his way out soon after.

To conclude, I often found, especially in my younger years, that I was wrong, happily wrong.

Losing Out on a Top Job

I did not always win the job that I wanted, when I wanted it. Sometimes the stars just did not align for me, but they did for someone else.

Eight years ago, as I was busy filling up my plate at a dinner buffet, a headhunter called and asked for my resume. He went on to tell me how big the bank was. I got excited about the opportunity. Then, there was zero news from him; he ghosted me. It turned out that he had a family emergency and never gave my resume to the owner. It took long to forgive him, but I already have. It is not easy to deal with such disappointment.

There is temptation to rationalize such losses. No one wants to admit defeat. But it is a setback, period. You accept it, and deal with it. And I don't mean by sour-graping.

You may have lost to a better-prepared person. You may not have the skills being sought. You may have been deemed not ready enough. If I were you, I would do the following:

1. Deliver: Performance is almost always a primary consideration.

2. Keep Learning: Build the skills you need for the target job.

3. Check Out the Competition: Understand their strengths.

4. Find an Honest Broker: Assess your chances compared to other candidates.

5. Establish Relationships: Connect with decision-makers.

If you can't do all five, at least do the first two.

Nowadays, when there are more senior positions available, you will just have to wait for your turn. However, the higher the job, the lesser your chances. At a certain point, you may simply have to move somewhere else.

Let me go back to my initial story. Three years later, I was invited to have dinner with the bank's owner. I still am in the same bank 6 years after.

When People Don't Cooperate

I had a session with a mentee who complained about colleagues being neglectful during group activities. Free riding starts quite early, even in elementary school. You then find them in college during team projects, in post grad, and in the office.

There are those whose definition of being smart means going through life with the least amount of effort. I have no problem with them as long as they do not ride on the effort of other people, or do not grab credit.

What to do? Have a chat with them to express the group's requirements. If peer pressure does not work or they stay invisible, remove them. Give them the least crucial parts of the project. In case they don't deliver, just chop off the section and their name from the group.

Do not overthink or overfeel. You are not responsible for them after you have done the minimum reminders and consideration. Best they learn their lesson early. It might be the best favor you can give them.

You have to choose whom to please. You cannot be everything to everyone. This is marketing 101. If you try to please all, you end up pleasing no one. You must choose your preferred market segments. This works for human relationships as well. Choose the ones most important to you. Care about how they think, ask for their opinion.

Whether you like it or not, some people will be difficult. You may not even know why; they just are. If they are not in your "preferred market segment," then just be civil and keep them out of your view.

It becomes complicated when the difficult person happens to be a senior. It happened to me in the early part of my banking career. To be fair, he was nasty to almost everyone else and his rudeness was the cause of his early exit. It turns out someone higher was just waiting for him to make a mistake.

Polarized and Stuck in a Gridlock

What if you work in a company where people are split into two sets of opposing views and are unwilling to compromise? What if the debate has become personal, resulting in name-calling? What if each side spends all their time with like-minded colleagues in an echo chamber, causing people to dig in and double down on their beliefs instead of reaching out to the other side?

The result is gridlock, even if the company is not split evenly down the middle. Much of the energy is wasted, and activities grind to a halt. This can lead to missed opportunities, decreased productivity, and a toxic work environment.

In my almost 40-year career, I have seen situations where groups within the company kept to themselves with their own set of leaders, like they were a tribe. Fortunately, they generally reached out to the rest of the organization and worked on deals together. There still was a network of friendships, of batchmates and classmates that crisscrossed the organization, tying it solidly together. Even if they were tribal, they had a strong feeling of belonging to the bigger organization. Citibank was a great example. I belonged to the treasury tribe. In fact, I still do, but at that point in my career, I was first a Citibanker.

Conversely, I was worried to find cliques who kept to themselves, often with an air of undeserved superiority and disdain for those who didn't belong, or those who chose to follow their different path regardless of what their bigger group's plan was. Loyalty was to individuals, not to the organization. This was unhealthy, and morale was adversely affected, leading to further divisions and a lack of unity. If the enemy is within, the battle is lost.

For an organization to grow and innovate, leaders have to work on building unity of purpose and goals. This has to be balanced by healthy, constructive debate. Leaders must encourage open communication and collaboration, breaking down barriers.

Unintended Consequences

When we develop new products or features, we often have customer problems or suggestions as the origin of those innovations. For example, the conversion of straight credit card purchases to installments via a few clicks on the mobile app (avoiding having to call our contact center) was ahead of local banks. Another innovation is the mobile app-based salary advance.

The upside to innovation is that customers are delighted, and we get more business. The downside is that we set the bar higher for ourselves in the eyes of the customer. When these new features have setbacks, we receive complaints, understandably so.

Sometimes, the reason behind the negative feedback is very different from what was originally intended. A classic example is the SMS message received when the supplementary cardholder makes a transaction. I am not referring to spouses checking shopping expenses. Not that. I am thinking about children.

When my younger son was still in university in another country, I would get an SMS whenever he took an Uber or Lyft. Based on the amount, I could surmise whether he went to see his cousins, his best friend, or his favorite eating place. That was not the important part. What was most valuable was when I got a notification of the second trip, as that meant he was safely back at the dorm.

A simple feature to prevent fraud just became a superb source of relief for me. That meant that if this feature malfunctioned, I would be extremely unhappy. Yes, even if the value I derived had zero to do with banking.

Customers do not always use our products the way we intended, but sometimes we hit a jackpot if it provides greater value.

Proving Persons Wrong

Arguing and convincing people aren't always worth the energy. It can be a waste of effort. However, if the issue has a major consequence, I will make time. If it is trivial, I may leave it alone.

How do I work this out?

1. Maybe I am wrong. Reassess my position, or find out more about the situation. Consult experts or research if needed.

2. Usually, if I know the person well enough, I would know if they are open or will listen to reason. If I don't, I will find out more about him/her. There might be some history or biases at work.

3. Approach the person in a more private or less public setting. Avoid spectators.

4. If you agree partially, mention those points of agreement. Then ask why he/she has that opinion. Be sincere, don't be condescending.

5. Make your points, don't be pushy. Use data if you have it. Give the other person time to chew on your position. He/she might need to sleep on it.

6. The other person might agree too quickly because you are the boss. Be discerning.

If he/she is right, and you are wrong, acknowledge. If you sense that the other person is being stubborn or is digging in, your next move depends on your seniority. Exercise your seniority if you must, unless you want to give the person the chance to experiment (provided his/her reasoning is sound).

Finally, there will be teammates who never listen, even if reason is against them. They may insist on their experience or street smarts. I remember what one stand-up comedian once declared—that being street smart requires that the person IS smart.

Bowing Out Graciously

This may sound counterintuitive to some. The idea is that a sharp career ascent needs to be balanced with the ability to be productive until normal retirement age. Let me explain. Moving up very quickly like a rising star, something that sounds ideal and impressive, tends to make you miss important lessons, relationships and soft skills that would have formed a solid foundation to support your growth as a leader.

I first heard about this from Rodrigo Zorrilla, my former boss. I thought it made sense and was a timely reminder. A career-limiting move early in the game can threaten your ability to support your family, for example. A more solid base of skills helps you become resilient, and setbacks become temporary. In other words, balance ambition with patience. Use time wisely to prepare yourself for bigger tasks.

Unfortunately, there are times in your life when you realize it is not worth staying longer in a post. This happened to me twice in the past. Either you don't feel safe or welcome anymore, and/or you see your growth limited. Your duty to yourself and your loved ones outweighs your obligations to an organization.

When you make the decision to leave, you have to do so with grace. Dwell on the positives because there should be enough to fill up a letter of gratitude. I am sure you learned a lot. Even your current state of mind will help you grow.

The friends you made, if genuine, will be your friends forever. Many years later, people will remember the happy times you had with them. And they will not have any bitter feelings.

Stay positive. You will find new purpose in a new home. I did. Still here and loving it.

Second Thoughts About Second Chances

I pondered about this after our guest speaker, one of the top conglomerate CEOs in the country, shared a column he read recently that suggested mistakes limit future opportunities. At first glance, this seemed like a direct argument against the now popular idea that failure is part of success.

According to him, the column took a "realistic" view that mistakes, especially if large or committed early, can alter a career path. It seems logical to stress that, if the mistake has significant consequences, the original plans may now be less possible.

But to suggest that the individual will no longer be able to reach his objective is another matter altogether. To be fair, the columnist did not state or hint that. I think, if there is sincere learning, he/she can keep climbing even a different path, but upward. I surmise that our speaker had the same view as mine.

While we have real-life examples of those who found themselves constrained, we keep being inspired by those who were sidelined, but ultimately succeeded because they never lost the will to fight.

Which brings me to an opposite point – early easy success can also alter someone's trajectory. While it may not seem tragic initially, it deprives him/her of the chance to learn and build resilience while the cost of failure is still low.

What perhaps is best, is to have a balance between being too optimistic about failure, and taking the extreme negative view. And to not take our opportunities lightly. We do the best we can even if failure is a possibility.

Something to keep thinking about.

"

I think the last mark of a leader is leaving his company in great shape even when he walks into the sunset, whenever he pleases.

Chapter Four

Transformational Leadership

The new environment requires that CEOs be more dynamic, more informed, and more resilient than ever. The traditional playbook has become outmoded; we need to write a new one that addresses these challenges.

Transformational leaders are those who understand their business deeply, continually update their knowledge, and communicate persuasively. These attributes enable them to lead change effectively, ensuring their organizations not only adapt, but thrive in a constantly evolving environment.

Can You Drive Change?

In my three decades in banking, I've often found myself in positions, countries, or new institutions on the brink of significant transformation. Leaders are crucial because they drive change. Here are the key attributes I've identified as essential for leaders to be effective change agents. I have narrowed them down to just three.

First and foremost, a leader must possess a comprehensive understanding of the business and the industry they belong to. This means grasping market dynamics, customer segmentation, regulatory issues, industry trends, competitive landscape, and the nuances of their organization. This provides a solid foundation for informed decision-making, and identifies inflection points where the leader can trigger faster growth.

Second, a leader should be a perpetual learner. In an era where new technologies and trends emerge rapidly, staying updated is not just essential; it is existential. Seven years ago, I felt ignorant about all the data and digital developments happening around me. I sought out new information through formal education, industry conferences, and self-study. Lifelong learning keeps leaders ahead of the curve and sets a powerful example of intellectual humility for their team.

Third, being an effective communicator is vital. A leader must be able to sell their vision and strategy clearly to employees and other stakeholders. Persuasive communication involves not just speaking, but also listening and engaging with the team. It's about selling the plan, building buy-in, and inspiring others to follow. When team members understand and believe in the vision, they are more likely to be committed. Sometimes, this may require a rewrite of the company's vision and mission statements.

Lately, I have spent the holidays reading journals about digital transformation and adaptive leadership. What have not changed are prescriptions on the type of leadership demanded for next-gen CEOs and leadership teams if they are to thrive in the future.

One set requires soft skills—listening, encouraging healthy debate, building a learning organization, breaking down silos in favor of collaboration, giving up old ways of control, among others. Traditional culture, especially in countries where there is a wide power distance, will need to radically transform as tasks and the manner of working have already changed.

Another set of skills requires knowledge of technological developments. For the leadership team to formulate a new vision, the team needs to learn current technology (code, get certified!), recruit to acquire expertise, and anticipate future trends.

But where do we go to get a better read on the future?

I have found visiting financial technology festivals as an important part of the process as you can see emerging technology all in one place. First, the Singapore FinTech Festival is the best in the region (and, I think, the best globally) because of a thriving ecosystem and aggressive government support. Second, advanced technology companies have laboratories that they have opened up to customers, which could be worth the trip. These are part of their marketing strategies and could serve as a source of valuable feedback. Next, visit other banks in neighboring countries that are more advanced and learn from them. Finally, choose technology companies to collaborate with as you can get first dibs on their new ideas if you are their preferred partner.

Attempting to be an adaptive and innovative leader during this stage of massive industrial and business transformation can be a position of extreme discomfort. However, I suggest that you view it as a present, because leaders have the privilege of implementing radical change that their organizations need to reinvent and outperform.

Finally, leaders must adjust, even abandon, current business models to exploit improvements while building new and innovative ones to explore future opportunities.

Becoming a Challenger Bank

Our industry has already been disrupted. We are caught between powerful incumbents on one side and innovative, fast-moving wallets and payments specialists on the other. The banking giants can deploy the fast-follower strategy; the fintechs are mixed, with two of them belonging to deep-pocketed conglomerates with captive customer bases.

Instead of resisting change, we must continue to embrace disruptive technologies and incorporate them into our business models. Some old skills or sources of competitive advantage (read: branches) may start to become partially obsolete.

Focusing on what we do best can be a powerful strategy. For us, it is customer service. Despite complaints (or because we address them), we rate highest in customer service according to surveys. We will keep doubling down on this, but we will also use new technologies to get even better at it and stay cutting-edge.

We are exploring new markets and product lines that can take advantage of our AI- and digitally reinforced skills and domain expertise. By moving into new opportunities, we reduce our dependence on traditional markets and go after new ones.

Continuous investment in people is crucial as it leads to better research and development. By staying at the forefront of innovation, we can develop new products and services that meet evolving customer needs.

Collaborating with fast-moving startups has provided us with access to new technologies and markets. We can accelerate our growth and innovation efforts.

All of the above are focused on enhancing customer experience. A superior customer experience across selected priority segments differentiates us from competitors and fosters long-term engagement.

Adopting these strategies allows us to respond effectively to disruptive forces, maintain our competitive edge, and thrive as a challenger bank in a rapidly evolving financial industry.

I've seen firsthand how embracing change can lead to incredible growth and innovation. It's been inspiring to watch our team adapt and excel in the face of challenges. By staying committed to our vision and supporting each other, we can continue to make a meaningful impact in the industry.

Rock Star CEOs

I have always been fascinated by business rock stars, from the time automakers like Iacocca and DeLorean showed up, then followed by Welch and Ghosn. There is one thing common among these stars: their companies did not do as well after them.

Thankfully, there are those who made sure their successors thrived after their departure. Technology companies such as Microsoft and Apple are outstanding examples. And JP Morgan's namesake bank continues to thrive under another rock star more than a century after he saved US banking.

Rock star CEOs are charismatic, high-profile leaders who are often written about and praised for their bold visions and transformative leadership. However, there are both potential benefits and significant risks associated with such leaders.

On the plus side, rock star CEOs are often associated with driving innovation and accelerated growth. They attract top-tier talent, creating an environment for breakthroughs. They can also be effective brand ambassadors. Moreover, they can be powerful motivators, inspiring their management teams and employees to undertake radical and transformational tasks.

However, all these benefits must be balanced with a strong awareness of the associated risks. Bold strategies must be supported by a robust risk management culture. The leadership bench must be strong, with potential successors being groomed to take over when the leader retires. Over-reliance on a single charismatic leader can be problematic when the CEO retires, as it can leave the company vulnerable.

Companies should focus on building sustainable strategies that do not solely rely on the vision of one individual. Developing a capable leadership team is a key step in this process. By leveraging the experience of established professionals and nurturing the potential of emerging talent, companies can create a robust and resilient organization capable of thriving long after the CEO has left the stage.

The organization is more important than its leader.

I've seen how fostering a culture of collaboration and continuous improvement can make a real difference. It's about prioritizing long-term goals and building a legacy of success. When everyone works together, the organization becomes stronger than any one leader.

Leadership Capital

There are leaders who utter a few words and everyone follows without hesitation. Such was Major Richard "Dick" Winters of the 101st Airborne, if you watched the series *Band of Brothers*, which I did three times.

Is this possible in the business setting, the leader barking an order? In the trading room, perhaps. Maybe not that dramatically, but it happens when the leader has maximum credibility. How then does the leader earn that "exalted" position? Is it even the preferred style of leadership?

Based on my readings and my observation of leaders that inspired me the most in my career, the primary factor is the leader's consistent record of results. Clear plans, diligent execution, goals achieved. The more difficult the challenge, the faster the leader earns leadership capital.

Second, he raises the standard, leading by example in work ethic, and in gaining new skills. He puts himself in harm's way. Third, empathy in communication. He explains what needs to be done to make sure everyone understands. Finally, resilience. Seeing your leader recover and rise is inspiring.

I prefer a collegial, participatory way of decision-making because that is how we get the benefit from diverse points of view, and the rest of the team learns. But there are times when, well, time is of the essence and the leader has to call the shots, pronto.

In an article by Schweiger, Stouten and Bleijenbergh (2018) entitled, *A System Dynamics Model of Resistance to Organizational Change: The Role of Participatory Strategies*, they suggested the concept of a social credit loop that "reduces participatory strategies whenever sufficient trust towards the change agents has been accumulated."

The accrued trust in the leader gains immediate support and avoids resistance. They, however, warn that this be used sparingly; otherwise, it will deplete the store of trust. What I will add is that, after the incident, the leader gathers the team and explains his decision.

Insights from Jamie's Visit

Jamie Dimon, the CEO of JPMorgan Chase, visited the country recently. I had the unique privilege to join a dozen bankers listen to him for one and a half hours while hundreds of JPM employees waited outside the conference room.

Jamie is the closest thing to a rock star in global banking. His bank's employees are justifiably proud of him. And many Citibankers view him as the one that got away. Naturally, I asked him about the circumstances behind his leaving and he gave us the unfiltered story. But I would rather write about his insights into banking and markets, which I also shared with my management team.

The first lesson was the importance of listening to customers. In an era where digital transformation is often prioritized, Jamie emphasized the importance of customers over current thought. If customers express a desire for physical branches, open them, even if it contradicts the prevailing digital dogma. This has resulted in good deposit growth for them. I noticed that their strategy actually consisted of closing a number but opening more, probably following demand data. Another interesting insight was the necessity for governments to instill fiscal discipline. With the increasing demand for funding in other areas such as renewable energy, it is imperative to start reducing deficits. Failure to do so could result in elevated interest rates in the future, which would have negative implications for the economy.

Investing in people and their continuous retraining is another cornerstone of Jamie's philosophy. In a rapidly evolving business landscape, it is essential to equip employees with the skills and knowledge they need to adapt and thrive. He mentioned AI several times, and the large number of projects they are undertaking.

Lastly, Jamie, a known supporter of blockchain technology but not crypto, advocated for ongoing investment in innovation to maintain a competitive edge.

In conclusion, his visit and his insights demonstrate why JPM has accomplished much during his leadership. There has been continuing talk about his succession. I think the last mark of a leader is leaving his company in great shape even when he walks into the sunset, whenever he pleases.

The King of Nothing

There was once a time when the CEO was like a king. He made decisions solely, and sometimes held power over the Board of Directors, especially if he/she was also the Chairperson.

That has changed. As governance standards tightened, the Chair and CEO jobs have been split, and the roles delineated, particularly for highly regulated companies. Governance advocates, which include institutional investors, have also encouraged this transition.

Even founders have stepped down. According to a Harvard Business Review study, only half the founders stay after a few years, and this wasn't always voluntary (Wasserman, 2008). The enlightened ones hire professional managers, or sell their start-ups. One of my mentees did exactly that, and he was happier afterward.

Companies have become much more complex to run in the digital and AI age where new competencies are demanded. Running and growing a company is different from founding one. The CEO must learn to work with his/her leadership team.

Mine in RCBC consists of experts in various facets of banking. Decision-making is collegial, especially for strategic and high-consequence matters that need to be discussed and debated thoroughly. Differing opinions are encouraged but have to be defended. Consensus has become the norm.

Naturally, there are still times when the buck stops with me, and I am comfortable making the call if it happens to be within one of my areas of expertise. But I do it usually after a small group consultation. Even an issue I might be confident about can serve as a learning experience for others.

Finally, I am reminded of the movie *The Boys in the Boat* (Clooney, 2023), about a junior varsity rowing team that won gold in the 1936 Berlin Olympics. In the closing scene, a young boy asked his grandpa how much he liked rowing an eight-man crew, to which the old man answered that they rowed as one.

Goals, Growth, and Glory

There is more to the RCBC story than our achievements in digital banking. The mission in 2019, which my leadership team chose to accept, was to bring the bank back to number five in 5 years.

We worked out a clear plan, but I thought the slogan was crucial. All over Facebook, when we did our posts, our hashtag was #fightto5.

Regaining lost glory meant so much to RCBC bankers. I thought I understood the emotional foundation behind the campaign, but I underestimated it. Severely. Thankfully, I eventually learned but in an unexpected way. You see, every week, I receive requests for hiring officers, and the forms detail personal backgrounds.

As I read more papers, I found out that over 70% of our employees come from families whose parents never reached college. A quarter of the fathers were drivers, an eighth farmers, and the rest were construction workers or were in similar jobs. Most mothers were housewives, some tending a *sari-sari* store or market stall.

That was when regaining our past glory started to mean more to me than just financials. Getting the bank into growth mode again would put careers back on track and provide advancement opportunities.

Our officers and staff are breadwinners. We employ 6,000, but are responsible for 30,000 when we include parents and siblings.

What happened was remarkable. We grew significantly faster than our peers across almost all measures, and we climbed a spot almost yearly. By December 2022, 1 year ahead of schedule, we were back at number five among all privately owned banks. This year alone, credit card balances are growing at over 50%, and auto and home loans over 20%, significantly faster than the industry.

Goals must mean something deep for employees. Result in pride restored. Careers growing again. Be able to support their families as the bank does better.

Soft Skills Are Exponential

We used to refer to this idea as "character," but it wasn't enough of a descriptor, so the term "EQ" became common. To differentiate the desired types of skills from technical, mechanical, analytical and artistic skills, they were referred to as soft skills.

When I Google soft skills, I see that various consultants have their own lists of five or seven or eight. I decided to write my own which I am convinced are the traits relevant in today's business setting characterized by rapid transformation and digital disruption.

These soft skills do not include "leadership skills" per se, but they all add up to what I think leaders need in their tool kit.

Here they are:

1. Ability to Inspire: Inspiration yields extraordinary results. An inspirational leader is vulnerable, authentic, and insightful. He/she also demonstrates tough empathy. He/she cares, but demands.

2. Persuasion: Digital and business transformation requires leaders who can convince stakeholders of new and radical strategies, and the massive effort and investments prescribed.

3. Courage: Change is often opposed; change can be scary. The leader needs to manage through uncertainty.

4. Teamwork and Collaboration: No one leads alone. The leader gets the best out of his team. This requires listening, brainstorming and buy-in.

5. Problem-solving: A leader needs to fix issues. The new method of design thinking means you need to pay close attention to customer feedback, and identify and solve root causes of problems.

6. Resilience: You need to rise from wrong, recover from ridicule, and redeem yourself from failure.

Hard skills can get you far and you definitely need to have them, but soft skills will get you further.

Management Offsites: Unplug, Unwind, and Unite

There is no unanimous opinion about team-building activities as some people think it is a waste of money, but management offsites hold immense value for me. They foster focused discussions on specific themes in a distraction-free environment. Stepping away from the daily business-as-usual allows leaders and teams to engage in strategic thinking.

Not all offsites are created equal, but preparation is key. Ours require thorough pre-work. Teams, whose composition is deliberately chosen, need to invest time in addressing identified issues, creating possible strategies, and gathering relevant data. Rather than starting from scratch, the prep work ensures that discussions are informed, efficient, and productive.

The relaxed atmosphere encourages everyone to share ideas freely, building stronger interpersonal relationships. This is one of the significant benefits of management offsites: the opportunity for team bonding. In a less formal setting, colleagues can engage in open and honest conversations, leading to a richer exchange of perspectives.

For a CEO, these offsites offer a unique vantage point to observe personal dynamics at play. Watching them collaborate on a challenging task provides valuable insights into their working relationship, and the rapport that develops. Facilitating positive interactions can lead to more cohesive and high-performing teams.

Additionally, offsites provide a chance to address any underlying issues that might not surface in the regular work environment. A candid discussion after dinner or after a round of drinks might reveal some concerns that were previously unvoiced. By creating a safe space for dialogue, leaders can identify and address potential conflicts or areas of concern, ultimately strengthening the overall team dynamic.

So, next time you're planning an offsite, think of it as an investment in your team's future. But avoid team-building activities without business brainstorming; they are a waste of money.

When Running Out of Ideas

There are times when the team just runs out of creative juices. How do you pump up the volume? Is it like squeezing something from stone? Try these:

1. Get your data scientists to pore over data and pick out counterintuitive trends. For example, how many customers use other banks' credit cards? Which supposedly weak segments actually exhibit good repayment behavior? Show your teams information which they do not know, or better yet, disprove their beliefs.

2. Study a top competitor. Figure out how you can beat their products and features. Try to understand their intentions. Reverse engineer, even mentally. Competitive strategy has a way of igniting the primal brain.

3. Have speakers from other industries that have done well in specific functions. One of the best marketing lessons I got came from skincare, when the company's digital marketing lead shared stories about how they won customers. It changed my view about social media fatigue.

4. Visit a client and immerse yourself in their process. Ask what they like about your competitors. Inquire about their wish list. Check the report on complaints. Do a root cause analysis on the main issues.

5. Spend time with young people and ask them about their banking habits. These conversations tend to be quite revealing.

Or have the team engage in any totally unrelated activity. Maybe all they need is to recharge. Or sleep. They may need to dust off cobwebs in their brains.

With rare exceptions, I have realized that I cannot dream about things or ideas unless they are inspired by something I have seen or read about before. The same is true with creativity and innovation.

Two-Speed Digital Transformation: Excerpts from a Keynote Speech

Digital and technical skills are mandatory. However, it did not take long for me to realize that apart from digital literacy, two other points were more important. First, transformation is about harnessing the energy of people – our leaders and employees. Second, innovation should have the customer as the object of our obsession.

HR established a digital academy and started focusing on customer experience, beginning with 30 seniors being certified as customer experience (CX) professionals by Dublin-based CX Academy, and the formation of a CX Council that, apart from championing CX, focused on tracking and solving customer complaints.

Middle management leaders went through design thinking workshops that, beyond being customer-obsessed, encouraged collaboration among individuals from various parts of the bank while working on solutions to customer problems. This facilitated bonding in the trenches.

How did we convince the entire bank? We first focused on a small portion of the bank, or a vanguard.

We employed a two-speed strategy where the vanguard ran very fast ahead of everybody else. We prioritized and supported three digitally motivated groups – digital banking, data science, and technology – and they built a new app, created new digital services, and wowed everyone else with new capabilities.

The three groups provided the proof of concept, convinced everyone that we were capable of making the grade, and their successful projects won us our first Best Digital Bank Award. Within months, we had more digital supporters, especially the branch officers, around the bank. And most of our employees caught up with the pioneers, at least in their level of enthusiasm as shown in their Facebook posts.

Finally, the digital leader is first an evangelist. My leadership team and I went around the country conducting town halls, explaining the strategy in detail and how exactly we would achieve our goals.

We shared success stories and highlighted the tangible benefits of our digital transformation efforts. Engaging directly with employees helped build trust and enthusiasm for the changes ahead. By fostering open communication and addressing concerns, we ensured everyone felt included in our journey toward becoming a leading digital bank.

nEver Stand Alone

Part Two

The Quantitative Leader

"

Even with the
abundance of
data, only with
the right skills
will we be able to
draw meaningful
insights.

Chapter Five

In Numeris Veritas

In numbers, the truth.

As we ushered in 2025, I sent my warm zero-degree greetings from Samarkand and Bukhara, two historic hubs along the Silk Road and legendary centers of old empires. They were also birthplaces of breakthroughs in medicine and mathematics. They have the right to claim they helped make the human race more naturally intelligent (NI).

Samarkand, with its stunning architecture, was a beacon of intellectual exchange. Here, scholars like Al-Khwarizmi developed the foundations of algebra and algorithms (named after his Latinized name), revolutionizing mathematics.

Math Meets Meat

At 13, I embarked on a summer research apprenticeship. Alongside 15 high school peers, I found myself at UP Los Baños, assigned to Animal Husbandry. My peculiar project: determine the optimal combination of chevon (goat meat) and pork for creating the most delectable sausages. You see, goat meat takes getting used to, and mixing with pork was the approach taken to make it acceptable. This was an adventure into the science of taste and texture, peppered with hypothesis testing.

Life at the men's dorm was a new experience. Each day began with a 2-km walk to the laboratory, where the real work started. I didn't actually make the sausages; my laboratory mentor did that. She prepared various sausage blends, adjusting the ratios of chevon to pork.

My role? The rigorous testing that followed. We recorded every detail: flavor profiles, texture, aroma, and overall acceptability. These data were organized into a randomized complete block design—a statistical method I'd only begun to grasp. I spent days doing the calculations by hand. We had no computers then. I can't recall exactly, but our null hypothesis would have been that the combination of chevon and pork would not affect the sausages' acceptability.

In this design, each block represented different meat ratios, and treatments were randomized to ensure unbiased results. Patterns emerged, revealing which blends were favored. Hypothesis testing played a crucial role, providing a structured approach to accept or reject our initial assumptions based on statistical evidence.

Despite not being the most thrilling topic, the approach and scientific method mattered more. By the end of the month, we'd identified the most acceptable chevon-pork combination and gained invaluable hands-on experience in scientific research.

I later presented our findings during graduation rites, another proud moment. Then, it was back home for my junior year, carrying a treasure trove of knowledge.

Algorithmic Leaders Coding

Over several days, under the mentoring of my senior data scientists, my leadership team took another deep dive into data science. Previously, data workshops and AI certifications from e-learning were mandatory. This time, it was hands-on. They learned and experienced coding using the Python language while going through the fundamental processes of data analytics.

It was important to start with appropriate business questions and hypotheses about the data to be collected. What followed were data preparation and wrangling. And no, I am not referring to the old rival of Levi's. Wrangling involves cleaning and fixing data to make it ready for analysis and decision-making.

This afternoon, I enthusiastically watched them present their capstone projects across various customer segments. I saw charts, I saw tables of recency-frequency-monetary value analytics, and I saw data-driven strategies. They were definitely competitive, and their domain expertise in their specializations was evident.

Of course, I wasn't expecting them to become scientists in such a short period of time. The objective was to further expose them to the exciting world of analytics so they understand the power of the partnership between domain expertise and a business-focused data science team. The data scientists also learned from this experience.

I have always been keen on ensuring that decisions and strategies were, as much as possible, based on data-driven insights rather than guesswork and "based on my experience" alone. Today, I saw an increased application and appreciation for this approach.

After all, this was not just a coding class but a step toward being algorithmic leaders who have the capability to understand the structure of algorithms, harness them to solve business problems, think computationally, and cultivate a curious and innovative mindset.

Serendipity and Statistics

Almost exactly 2 years ago, I met this remarkable young woman who was contemplating pursuing a master's degree in data science at the Asian Institute of Management. She wasn't sure how to make it work because she had a promising career in investment management, and a full-time program meant giving up a good salary.

She got lucky—or maybe not—because I looked forward to meeting her anyway. Seated beside her was a trustee of AIM. Me. In a stroke of serendipity, I happened to know that AIM was about to announce a part-time program in 2 weeks. I shared this information with her, along with other details about the process.

Encouraged, she decided to apply. I kept tabs on her application and knew ahead of time that her application went well. She was highly qualified as, apart from self-learning advanced math (which was brutal), she brought to the classroom her domain expertise in investment management. Fast forward 2 years, and she is now nearing the final lap of the course.

Months ago, while on a group tour in Tuscany, she saw me sitting alone at a table, deep into a Zoom recording and scribbling numbers in my notebook while multitasking over a bag of chips. Recognizing the concepts I was working on, she came over to check out my notes. To her amusement, I was working on two-tailed hypothesis testing of two samples—something she was now well-versed in thanks to her studies. It's funny how the tables have turned, and I'm now learning statistics while she is mastering it.

Reflecting on this encounter, I can't help but marvel at how our paths crossed in that airline lounge one evening. Her decision to pursue further education in data science has not only broadened her career choices, but has also become a point of connection for us. I will be proud to watch her during her graduation.

Grab the Tables

One morning, I woke up early to re-read a second article from a management journal on advanced technology. As suggested by Professor Jammu Francisco, the first thing I did was go straight to the tables, often tucked away in the appendices. This approach made perfect sense.

Reflecting on my MBA days, I recalled how we always dived straight into the numbers, equipped with our calculators and markers. When I receive an annual report from any of the clubs or associations I belong to, my first move is always to check the financial statements; they tell the story quickly and efficiently. If anything catches my attention, I go to the notes and other details.

For instance, the tables from a technical article on artificial intelligence clearly showed which factors mattered most, which were irrelevant, and even which were counterintuitively negative. They also indicated whether the information was statistically significant. In layman's terms, they allowed you to cut through the bull and get straight to the insights and the facts.

An hour after this study session, I found myself in the hotel breakfast restaurant. Interestingly, the first thing I did was grab a table—literally. It seemed more important than the food itself. In some countries, like Singapore, grabbing the table is almost an art form. It's all about securing that perfect spot, whether it's for the best view or just proximity to the breakfast buffet. Similar to diving into financial tables, snagging that prime spot can make or break your dining experience.

As I settled into my table, I couldn't help but draw parallels. Just as tables in management journals provide clarity and insights, grabbing a table at the restaurant ensured a smooth and enjoyable start to the day. Both acts require a strategy, a keen eye for detail, and an understanding of what truly matters.

Aha Moments in Analytics

I used to think that my three decades as a banker—and those of my leadership team—put us in a good position to make good banking decisions. However, it turned out that many of our long-held, traditional beliefs were not accurate. Data analytics, even in its diagnostic form, showed us the truth.

Instead of making assumptions about what the customer is doing or will do, we study the data on actual customer behavior.

As Eric Sandosham, a former Citi colleague, once wrote, giving data science a seat in the company's strategy meetings ensures that discussions are honest.

Here are a few examples:

1. Branch and ATM locations are now guided by points of interest and actual behavior of customer segments, in addition to the addresses of affluents/businesses and PDIC data. The approval process is quicker and drama-free.

2. On cash management, instead of product management setting the price and relationship managers complaining, we based pricing on actual customer usage/behavior evidenced by numbers and effect on cross-sell.

3. On consumer products, offerings are based on the total relationship that results from the introduction of the products, again as evidenced by data.

I caution readers to be aware of the difference between correlation (the rooster announcing the morning sun) versus causation (the earth's rotation). This matters greatly, but data scientists will be excited to assist provided you explain your objective and the context.

I encourage you to question your existing practices, especially if it "feels wrong" and use analytics to better understand the situation. You will be happy to find the truth.

Relationships and Connections

Every Saturday afternoon, my classmates and I hunt for relationships. To put it bluntly, we do not start to engage unless we know the target's statistics. Thankfully, we often see success within minutes. This is like speed-dating, the type where you find potential correlation partners for variables.

This efficiency is largely due to the fact that we use the right digital tools of the trade. We Excel at it. Our mentor's wealth of experience and insight guides us through the process.

At first glance, the objects of our interest may seem random, scattered, and disorganized. However, once we learn to forgive their flaws and adjust our confidence level, they often lead us down a promising path. Perhaps these imperfections are there to maintain some mystery, a bit of error?

Why do we keep at it? It's because those little things really do matter. Little things can turn into big things when they press the right buttons, keeping the relationship alive and well. The small details often hold the most significance and reveal intimate insights.

Sadly, these new relationships can sometimes lack substance, or even be shallow. This can be frustrating, but it is all part of the learning process. And then there are times when it is too good to be true, and red lights start flashing. The factors appear quite aligned, almost like an ideal match, but then we realize they are contrived.

As we continue on our quest for connections, we realize that each failure or success contributes to our understanding. We are warned not to torture the data because, at some point, it will confess to anything.

I have learned to look forward to each Statistics and Data Science class under Prof. Corinne Burgos every Saturday afternoon. Even with the abundance of data, only with the right skills will we be able to draw meaningful insights.

Are You a Data-Driven Leader?

As Prof. Corinne loves to remind: "Data is everywhere, insights are rare."

Here are some ideas on how to elevate your data game. They have been enhanced by my recent studies in analytics, and by my chief data scientist Pam Cabudoy.

1. Understand Customers

Beyond traditional segments, start by creating customer personas using clustering tools and network analysis to identify sub-segments that have very similar behavior and/or are connected. Once done, you can analyze these personas more deeply. AI machine learning models can predict which customers are more inclined to purchase certain services. There is actually much more to do, but it is sufficient to say that scientific targeting or leads generation is more efficient than having your sales team contact (and possibly annoy) every single customer in their lists.

Sentiment analysis allows us to quickly aggregate social media feedback with a positive or negative score. But I prefer to dive further and use AI tools to find out what exactly customers are worried about, so we can do something about it.

2. Improve Efficiency

We have always been keen about branch queues as it is high in the list of complaints. Our team runs a quantitative capacity study that simulates branch queues, which they review regularly. We do the same for our call center where we drill down response rates, first call resolution percentages, and the trend of top complaints. This has allowed us to prioritize the more pressing issues. Visualizing data helps a great deal as it is easier to understand the situation.

3. Manage Risks

This part has been quantitatively driven even in the 80s, at least on the market risk side where we ran simulations, and on consumer credit risk where we first employed math wizards. We sliced the customer base into various segments from high risk to low risk, to find acceptable cutoffs. By analyzing historical data on loan defaults, market trends, and economic indicators, we can develop predictive models to forecast expected credit losses. We are particularly keen on monitoring the differences of default trends across years (we call them vintages, like wine), to identify early warning signals.

4. Sharpen Strategy

Data allow leaders to measure performance against strategic goals. They have customized dashboards that make it easier to track KPIs and identify areas for improvement. In addition, we question traditional practices, which I love to refer to as hypotheses, and use data to confirm or reject them. Rejected hypotheses are exciting because they give rise to new practices that allow us to outperform competition.

To close, data empower leaders to make sharper decisions that drive success.

You Can Handle the Truth

In modern business, you cannot be a data-driven business leader if you don't dive into the numbers, or if you readily accept them without diligence. We are at an age where data are everywhere. Even better, the abundance is accompanied by faster computers and amazing analytics tools. Therefore, there is no excuse for shallow interpretations.

Here's what I have learned about how we can do better:

1. First, tell a story using the numbers. Focus on the most important parameters that have the biggest impact on the business. Keep it simple and tight.

2. Visualize data. Avoid plain tables. Use charts, graphs and other tools which highlight trends even before the presenter opens his mouth. Never accept just the averages as they can even mislead. Show the distribution of the values, then go after the outliers.

3. Analyze the trend over a period of time, and compare this with historical data, the budget, and industry performance. It is always nice to see the business beating previous year's numbers while paying attention to seasonality (like year-end surges).

4. But there is no joy in doing well if the industry is doing better. If a competitor is showing admirable progress, study their numbers in as much detail as you can.

5. Explain the specific action plans that contributed to the trend. Show proof that those actions caused the trend. Be careful of correlation versus causation.

6. Break the performance across product and customer segment cuts to see the trend in each category. The results may be mixed; pay attention to the laggards.

And, finally:

7. If you think something is wrong in the presentation, challenge the data. Are the samples representative of the population? Use hypothesis testing to determine that the conclusion presented is valid.

Remember: data are your best friends, but only if you treat them right. Dive deep, question everything, and never settle for surface-level insights. After all, in the world of business, the curious minds find the gold nuggets hidden in the data mines.

Keep It Simple

As a physics major, I spent 4 years calculating solutions. As a physics lecturer, I had to concoct new problem sets since old quizzes were often shared among students as reviewers. As an aside, I started using the movie *Dune* as a setting for falling weapons and other scenarios; I found out last year that the faculty has resumed this creative practice as the movie was remade. We did what we could to entertain students.

As a derivatives structurer, I tinkered with potential client solutions. In all of these, I strived for one thing: elegance. Let me explain. When I say elegance, it has to be as simple as possible to some extent so that it becomes self-explanatory. And it has to be accurate to a significant degree such that the effort of additional complexity will not result in any worthwhile incremental accuracy and additional intellectual stimulation. I used my shortcuts to check the work of my teammates.

At the same time, it cannot be too simple as to limit its application and relevance. I remember I was once asked by seniors, who calculated a long-term transaction using what turned out to be a simplified FX forward formula, to reconcile their calculations. I found the required adjustment and saw a few months later that newly published books actually used a slightly longer formula that included the adjustment. The new version proved to be highly maneuverable. And yes—elegant.

Today, I reviewed my statistics homework and realized I broke the elegance rule. I went about solving one problem the convoluted way when the simple answer was actually right there under my very nose, generated by the software. The mistake was rushing to the solution without thoroughly digesting the problem. It happens.

In statistics, we are reminded to be frugal, meaning we employ the least amount of assumptions to explain a correlation. This makes sense because, in actual business practice, we prefer to focus our efforts on more important matters.

People Come First

Technology is not the most important thing. Otherwise, you can just buy it and immediately become successful. Technical skills can only get you to a limited distance.

People come first. And this is where digital leadership and cultural evolution become crucial.

Beyond the technical aspects, the digital leader is first an evangelist. A digital transformation exercise demands a massive amount of investment in technology and in people. The leader needs to persuade the Board and other stakeholders to support the required capital outlay and significant effort required, by presenting a credible transformation plan that will include new business models, expense reductions and future revenue streams.

Then the leader has to make it happen, through people.

As digital transformation will affect hundreds and thousands of jobs, the leader must go to town halls explaining how businesses will be affected, the benefits, and career growth for those who learn new skills.

Culture will need to change into one that is agile, customer-obsessed and collaborative. The leader will work with HR on cultural transformation initiatives, and celebrate small victories achieved by cross-functional teams, while ensuring these projects are focused on real customer problems, rather than pa-*pogi* (to look good) projects.

The leader will convince a new type of employee – data scientists, engineers, coders- that do not fit the traditional mold, to join the company, and then make them feel welcome. The leader also has to ensure that the data scientists live in a community that will embrace the power of analytics. And decisions should start to be driven by data and experimentation, instead of a senior person's experience and gut feel.

Given limited resources, the leader has to choose alternatives and opportunities that are consistent with the strategy. Priority has to be given to products that can be scaled up rather than those with limited potential.

Not everything will go as planned. The leader will keep the energy level high, remind everyone that failure is part of the process, quickly learn from it, and strive to get better.

It turns out that soft skills are more important than technical skills. A digital leader must work well with teams, be agile, listen to his colleagues, think critically, and more. Culture change cannot happen if the leader and the leadership team do not model the right behavior.

As we continue on our digital journey, let us remind ourselves of what we have known all along. Our best people, now digitally enabled, will remain our best assets.

"

They say birds of the same feather flock together, and in the world of numbers, that sentiment is particularly true.

Chapter Six

The Damn Truth and Statistics

The former British Prime Minister, Benjamin Disraeli, allegedly uttered the phrase "lies, damn lies, and statistics," suggesting that numbers can be manipulated in a way that misleads.

To be fair, I still see that happening nowadays, particularly during elections. But in business, I think we have sufficient controls in place.

Statistically Speaking

Sometime October 2024, I immersed myself in preparing for a long exam in our Statistics and Data Analysis course. My 18 classmates were focused on their notes and spreadsheets as well, so I was not alone in my misery; I had company. The topics covered included normal distribution, confidence intervals, hypothesis tests, goodness of fit, and independence tests.

Thankfully, we don't do calculations longhand, although we can. Excel has been, well, excellent because various calculators have been coded into that old tool. But we found a new ally in an open-source software called Jamovi. I had to learn this by myself after examples in class because, to my horror, my data scientists never heard of this novelty before. To be fair, this is pretty new, although superbly nifty.

Okay, I exaggerated about being miserable. I am not. Delving into these concepts for the first time has given me a newfound appreciation, maybe even affection, for stats, the stats team, and their potential for more strategic work. I realized that we can leverage their expertise for even greater impact.

There is more to this. Understanding election polls has become clearer, allowing me to distinguish between reliable data and misleading information. With pollsters set to appear in a few months, I now recognize the importance of accurate analysis and deliberate spin doctoring. I now can better appreciate why media trends from other countries, which were coopted locally, left me puzzled. My brain told me it didn't make sense, yet thousands insisted on it and declared they were ahead.

Reflecting on my senior year in university, I recall the simplicity of counting raised hands and tallying them. Statistics was just another subject to hurdle, sandwiched in my schedule between Optics and Electricity and Magnetism. One memorable day, I attended class after being jolted by 900 DC.

This journey has transformed my perspective on statistics, revealing its true power and potential. I am a fan.

A Statistics Enthusiast

In the past, I thought I was sufficiently numerical in my approach to doing business. I wanted to see charts, even asked for correlations and statistical data, and how many samples were used to check for significance. It turns out I was just scratching the surface. As one of my classmates quoted recently, a little knowledge can be dangerous. What might even be riskier is when no one else knows better and the squinting one-eyed becomes king.

In fact, writing about how to be better quantitatively puts me in a bit of peril. I am doing this anyway because I believe that, when I learn something new, it is my obligation to share what new skills I've found, especially if I enjoyed pondering about those concepts during our class. My objective is to turn my leader colleagues into the data scientist's best ally, and who will be in a better position to engage the data science team and maximize their effectiveness.

I will cover ten topics. We have used most of them in my company, while the others I found worthy of application.

1. Descriptive Statistics

This is fundamental for summarizing large amounts of data. It includes measures such as mean (average), median (middle value), mode (most frequent value), and standard deviation. I have seen leaders frequently simplify by just using the average. That practice hides a significant part of the story whenever the actual range of data is wide.

It is also important to note that not all data are quantitative. Some are categorical, like gender or civil status. You can calculate an average age but not an average gender. Not to worry, this is where bars and other charts come in handy. By visualizing data distribution, in addition to the descriptive stats, you can better understand your data. In fact, two samples with exactly the same stats can look totally different when charted. Our prof gave this in our exam to drive home the point.

For example, in monthly sales reports, descriptive statistics can summarize sales data. For instance, average sales per region can mark a cutoff that can identify the better performing regions from weak ones. But that can hide bad performance within good regions. To find out how individual salespeople are doing within each region, this is where the standard deviation can be useful, although it is better showing the distribution spread in visuals like through a box and whisker plot.

Visualizing Descriptive Statistics

When preparing reports, it is important to choose the most appropriate type of chart that will communicate the right story. Here are the more popular ones.

Pie Charts: It is very often used as it clearly shows proportions such as the composition of an investment portfolio. However, it has more limitations than advantages. It is difficult to optically compare slices, especially when there are many cuts. Depending on how the pie is drawn, proportions can be misleading. An alternative is a tile chart where the proportions are shown as rectangular boxes.

Bar Charts and Stacked Bar Charts: These are more effective when comparing quantities over several categories, as bar heights are easier to directly compare. You can also show how different components stack within each bar and how they move across time intervals. Alternatively, the bar components can be converted to ratios, doing a better job than pie charts. For example, a company can show quarterly accomplishment as the total bar height, while indicating the performance of all the product categories as different colors within the bar. Visually, the reader will be able to see how each category did over time.

Line Charts: Lines illustrate trends, for example, across revenue, expense, and income. The slopes of various lines can be compared to see which is growing faster, and the spread between them can indicate important metrics like net margins. It is simple but quite revealing. I also like to use lines as an overlay on bar charts. An interest rate trendline can be superimposed over bars showing loan or deposit volumes.

One of the most impressive charts I have ever seen was the rose chart prepared by Florence Nightingale (yes, the founder of modern nursing), to illustrate that most deaths of British soldiers were due to poor hygiene rather than battle wounds.

Make it as simple as possible, and easy to understand without further explanations. Indeed, a great chart replaces a thousand words.

2. RFM Analysis

Recency, frequency, and monetary (RFM) analysis segments customers based on their transaction behavior. We evaluate the customer's most recent transaction, how often the transactions happen, and the sizes. Customers can be grouped into categories based on the weighted scores for the three parameters.

The analysis identifies high-value customers, and marketing programs can be directed toward them to sustain loyalty. More crucially, those whose scores have come down—if they haven't done a deal lately for example—have to be watched as they might have started falling for another bank. Re-engagement activities need to be executed.

The first time I saw this concept used was in an oil company that had retail stations. The extensive database warned dealership owners if certain large customers were no longer loading their usual volumes, and might be refueling elsewhere.

3. Probability Distributions

Probability distributions describe how the values of a variable are distributed. These include the widely used normal distribution or the bell curve, binomial distribution and Poisson distribution.

The normal distribution is easier to imagine and is described by its mean and standard deviation. This has many uses in forecasting various business parameters based on historical data. In banking, it is employed in risk management, like when determining risk tolerance or investment returns. I particularly find it helpful when presented visually.

The binomial distribution, which models two outcomes, can calculate success rates in marketing or sales campaigns. The Poisson distribution can estimate the number of events occurring within an interval, like the number of customers arriving or phone calls received.

4. Expected Value Analysis

We did days of expected value analysis during my MBA. It is a theoretical construct for evaluating decision-making. It first quantifies the potential business outcomes of a decision. Then, using probabilities, it calculates the weighted average of all possible outcomes. It is useful for comparing alternative decisions.

For example, when considering a new market entry, we use expected value analysis to evaluate potential revenue outcomes based on different market conditions. By assigning probabilities to different conditions (e.g., high demand, moderate demand, and low demand), we calculate the expected revenue and decide whether the investment is worthwhile.

5. Interval Analysis

Interval analysis involves analyzing and comparing the ranges within which data points fall. It helps in understanding the variability and consistency of processes. By examining the intervals or ranges, you can identify patterns and deviations, enabling better process control.

A common sample usage is in quality control, where interval analysis is the basis for monitoring product specifications. By setting acceptable ranges for key metrics such as weight or dimensions, we ensure that products meet quality standards and identify any deviations promptly.

6. Regression Analysis

Regression analysis is one of the more frequently used tools. It quantifies the relationship between a dependent variable (the target) and one or more independent variables (the predictors). It is particularly useful for predicting future trends based on historical data.

Regression models, such as linear regression, can provide insights into how changes in one significant variable/predictor (e.g., advertising spend) affects the target variable (e.g., sales revenue). By analyzing historical data, we can determine the impact of marketing efforts on sales performance and optimize future marketing budgets. For example, a linear regression model might show that increasing advertising spend by $10,000 results in an average sales increase of $50,000.

7. Correlation Coefficient

The correlation coefficient measures the strength and direction of the relationship between two variables. It ranges from -1 to +1, where +1 indicates a perfect positive correlation, -1 indicates a perfect negative correlation, and 0 indicates no correlation. This is a very handy tool, as long as you remember that correlation does not prove that one causes the other.

For example, we can use correlation coefficients to analyze the relationship between customer satisfaction scores and repeat purchase rates. For instance, a correlation coefficient of +0.8 suggests a strong positive relationship, meaning that as customer satisfaction increases, repeat purchase rates also increase.

8. Hypothesis Testing

Hypothesis testing has been my newest favorite tool to evaluate previous assumptions and rules of thumb, and make informed business decisions going forward. This method allows you to draw conclusions about a population based on sample data. Common tests include t-tests (comparing means) and chi-square tests (comparing categorical variables). For example, you can test whether a new marketing strategy significantly increases customer engagement beyond just looking at the average and standard deviations.

Before fully rolling out a new promotional campaign, we conduct hypothesis testing to compare engagement levels between a test group and a control group. This helps us determine the campaign's effectiveness. If the resulting p-value is less than 0.05 (this comes out from the statistical calculations), we can conclude that the new campaign has a statistically significant impact on customer engagement.

9. ANOVA

Analysis of variance (ANOVA) is used to compare the means of three or more groups to see if they differ significantly. It's useful in experimental design and analyzing survey data. ANOVA helps determine whether any observed differences in means are statistically significant or just due to random variation.

This tool is useful in analyzing customer satisfaction surveys across different departments. This helps us identify which ones are performing well and which need improvement. By comparing the means of satisfaction scores, we can determine if the differences are statistically significant and take appropriate actions to address any issues.

10. Cluster Analysis

This tool groups similar data points together to identify patterns and insights within the data. It is commonly used in market segmentation, customer profiling, and identifying patterns in large datasets.

We use cluster analysis to segment our customer base into groups with similar purchasing behaviors. This helps us create targeted marketing campaigns and personalized experiences for each segment, improving customer engagement and loyalty. For instance, we might identify distinct clusters such as shoppers and travelers, allowing us to tailor our marketing strategies for each segment.

By integrating these statistical tools into our daily operations, we've been able to make better informed decisions, identify opportunities, and mitigate risks effectively. These tools have provided us with valuable insights, helping us stay ahead in a competitive market.

Do Leaders Live Longer?

Being a leader has its pluses, but it carries with it a significant burden of responsibility, which arguably increases stress levels. This led me to wonder whether leadership results in a shorter life span. Instead of philosophizing, I looked for research studies to enlighten me on this issue and found one written by Olenski, Abola and Jena in December 2015.

In their study, elected leaders lived 2.7 years fewer than runners-up (range of 0.6 to 4.8, with a 95% confidence level). Without adjusting for life expectancy during the election, the number was 4.4 years. This was based on national elections occurring in 17 countries: Australia, Austria, Canada, Denmark, Finland, France, Germany, Greece, Ireland, Italy, New Zealand, Norway, Poland, Spain, Sweden, the United Kingdom, and the United States. (For my friends familiar with statistics, the P value was 0.001. This was statistically significant.)

I thought that comparing winners and losers was fair as they had similar economic standing and access to medical care. There was another study that suggested politicians lived longer than the electorate, but I won't cover that.

The study by Olenski, Abola and Jena (2015), entitled "Do heads of government age more quickly? Observational study comparing mortality between elected leaders and runners-up in national elections of 17 countries," provides a compelling look at the impact of leadership on life expectancy. The findings suggest that the stress and responsibilities associated with leadership roles can indeed take a toll on one's health and longevity.

So, what now? I have been a corporate leader for most of the last 15 years. This suggests that I should be more conscious about my health issues compared to the next guy. Statistics of a related field are not in my favor, so I need to take heed.

Birds of a Feather

They say birds of the same feather flock together, and in the world of numbers, that sentiment is particularly true. When analyzing populations, the instinctive move is to calculate the average. It's the fastest way to get an idea of what's going on. However, relying solely on that number can be misleading. Averages have this sneaky way of swinging widely, especially in a large range, leaving us with more questions than answers.

Picture this: you're looking at a massive flock of birds. They're all over the place, and pinning down the average bird seems almost impossible. This scatter causes one crucial realization: the average, as a solitary measure, isn't useful and can even be downright misleading.

But then, you have a eureka moment. You decide to split the birds imaginarily into smaller, more manageable groups. Of course, you can't physically catch them all, but in your mind, you classify them by similar traits. This second look at the population reveals an insightful truth: they consist of several distinct groups. Birds of the same feather do indeed flock together. They exhibit similar behaviors, munch on the same seeds, and favor the same flight paths. Suddenly, the average becomes a useful tool.

Now, simplification is within reach. They are not a single uniform entity but thrive in clusters, each with its own story.

This realization brings me to a classic statistics joke. Two data scientists went hunting. As they approached a flock, they aimed and fired. Not having practiced, one shot a meter too far to the left, and the other missed by a meter to the right. They both shouted, "We got them!", and went to a bar to celebrate. The moral of the story? Averages can be deceiving, but understanding the diversity within the data can lead to true insights.

By taking that second look and recognizing the inherent groups within a population, we can finally simplify and understand the complexity of the data world. So, remember, it's often the birds of the same feather that tell the real story.

Quantifying Loyalty

Big businesses can learn a lot from salons and barber shops. Take Back Alley Barbershop along Bautista Road in Salcedo Village, Makati, for example. I go there every 2 or 3 weeks. More than just getting a regular cut, I linger a little longer for some extra "me time". Then, I tell my friends about my good experience. Sometimes, I even write about it— like I am doing now.

I consider myself a loyal customer. But how does this translate to big business? It can be challenging to track customers coming in and out of our shops and branches. What if someone hasn't visited in a month or two? Were they on vacation, or have they found another service provider?

Enter RFM analysis—Recency, Frequency, and Monetary value. Our data scientists use this method to measure customer loyalty. In barbershop terms: we should be concerned if we don't see Eugene within a month.

RFM analysis quantifies customer behavior by scoring three parameters— monetary value, count and recency of transactions. Customers are segmented for each parameter, usually by threes based on their distribution or by quartiles. Then, they are plotted in a 3x3 or 4x4 matrix, with monetary value on one side and a weighted score of recency and frequency. This way, it becomes visually clear which segments can be touched for certain actions. For example, a segment with high monetary value score but low in recency and frequency will be a target for retention efforts.

But there's more to it. How do we measure whether a customer is referring the barbershop to their friends? Referrals are a powerful acquisition tool! Data scientists use Network Analysis. By analyzing transactions, we can identify which customers are strong influencers. If the people connected to, and surrounding these influencers, have high RFM scores as well, then we've got a winning strategy.

Customer loyalty is invaluable, but it becomes even more precious when loyal customers become advocates and salespeople for your business. So, whether you're running a barbershop or a large bank, understanding customer loyalty through these methods can be a game-changer.

Curious About Linear Regression

As we will be spending four long sessions on regression, Prof. Corinne shared with us some historical trivia about its origin. Then I read up more about it online.

Sir Francis Galton, a first cousin of Charles Darwin, was a pioneer in the field of statistics. In one study, he measured the midpoint heights of couples (by multiplying a 1.08 factor to the female height to account for gender) and their children. He observed a fascinating trend: short parents tend to have children a bit taller than themselves, while tall parents had children who were a bit shorter. This phenomenon led to the coining of the term "regression," indicating that heights of children tended to move toward the population average. Contrary to what we practice now, regression originally did not refer to the fitting of a line on a scatter of points.

Simply put, regression is the same as reversion to the mean. Galton further calculated this regression to follow a ratio of two-thirds. This meant that if the parents' height differed (whether shorter or taller) from the average by 3 inches, the child's height would vary by approximately 2 inches from the population average. Children of short parents became less short, and children of tall parents became less tall.

Galton's work laid the foundation for regression analysis, which is very popular nowadays, and which unwittingly led to people immediately assuming wrongly that one caused the other. Just because two factors are highly correlated does not prove that one caused the other. I asked the prof how to prove causality, and she answered: "Do an experiment." For example, we can have roosters make their usual sound and see if it makes the sun rise. I am exaggerating.

Beyond his work on regression, Galton conducted an experiment on the power of prayer, which he concluded had no measurable effect. Many would disagree with this notion. Maybe it is immeasurable.

When Election Surveys Turn Out Wrong

I've always been a keen observer of polls, viewing them with a mix of interest and suspicion. To be fair, it's more of the former, but I've seen situations where the numbers were wrong—either deliberately or due to deeper, non-sinister reasons.

At the risk of oversimplification, polls rely on two main factors: first, that the pollster employs appropriate sampling methods to avoid bias; and second, that respondents actually reply and are truthful.

There is sufficient theory on how to conduct sampling properly that people can read up on. A significant pitfall can be the manner of conducting the poll. For example, using landlines as a method of contact can exclude certain segments of the population from the sample.

I'm more curious about certain behavioral reasons. There's Social Desirability Bias (SDB), for example. Simply put, when asked, people may answer in a way that casts them in a good light. For instance, if someone is surrounded by others who unanimously support a candidate, he/she might reluctantly go along during surveys but vote differently when casting the ballot.

If the candidate is controversial, supporters might hide their intentions, fearing social backlash. Yet, during voting, they might confidently select their candidate. I have other reasons why, controversial or not, I keep my choices to myself.

This phenomenon isn't limited to elections—it happens in the workplace as well, when assessing morale and issues. This is why maintaining a sufficient degree of anonymity is crucial.

Social desirability bias and other forms of response bias pose significant challenges to the accuracy of polls and surveys. The classic example mentioned in studies is the Bradley effect where the popular African American LA mayor was leading the polls when he ran for California governor. The election results were quite different. Read about it.

"

While AI has become a cornerstone of modern life, its true value lies in our ability to harness it for the greater good.

Chapter Seven

Unlocking Artificial Intelligence

In the 90s, my aunt called me out of the blue and asked if my cousin, who just graduated, could find employment as a filing clerk. I replied, to her surprise, that we no longer had filing clerks. I explained that memos were sent electronically, and that the act of filing was simply dragging the file to an electronic folder.

The same revolution is happening to chess. I follow the chess ratings of those with ELO ratings over 2700 (the super grandmasters). Machines have gotten much better, can beat the players, and are now being used for training and practice. Until when will we celebrate our chess stars?

Which professions will follow next?

Tinkering with AI

For a long time, I felt grossly inadequate when discussing AI. Sure, I come from a quantitative background. Sure, I took almost half a dozen certifications in data science, which included portions on AI. And sure, I even went back to a bit of Python coding, which was made easier because I used to program 40 years ago.

But unless I tinkered with numbers myself, I would always feel like a fraud and prefer that we listen to the AI experts themselves. I have spent a tremendous amount of time with my data scientists. This has allowed me to appreciate what they do and create a sustainable competitive advantage for our business groups.

However, I still felt like I was only a passenger in a sophisticated car. I can talk about the car, surely, and my friends and audience will listen. But I never drove the car.

This is why I appreciated "suffering" through the Statistics and Data Analysis course in the DBA program. The first week was a state of panic as I was reintroduced to software. I immediately fell for Excel's statistical tools and the amazing Jamovi open-source, R-based software, which was an analytics calculator on steroids. Before we knew it, in 4 months, we completed a two-inch thick book.

Then we found ourselves tinkering more with Jamovi, this time doing multiple regressions and logistic regressions, moving to the world of my data scientists. Now, I appreciate better how many of our models work. I have maneuvered a few samples in class myself to appreciate how to tweak models to improve predictive value. I reviewed for our final exam very willingly, like the time I first learned how to drive and savored odds-ratios, recalls and false positives. And now I, a bit more deeply, understand why it is imperative that my scientists know what the business objective is, because the models need to reflect that goal. The learning does not stop.

AI and Its Consequences

AI, like any transformative tool that came before it, brings issues. The difference is the issues are amplified in the case of AI. This is why we use it with our eyes wide open. Let me share some of the main ones:

Academic Issues: This reminds me of the time in the early 80's when calculators were forbidden. Then, computers were not allowed. Those two tools are now omnipresent in classrooms. A particular concern is that students use AI to write essays. There is even software that can assess the probability of whether a certain submission was written by AI, but with a statistical margin of error. If such a tool is used by faculty, it can be the equivalent of unfairly pronouncing someone guilty, or unfairly suspecting.

Bias and Fairness: If the data used to train AI models are biased, AI's predictions and decisions can also be biased, leading to potentially unfair outcomes. This is garbage in, garbage out. For example, it can classify certain customer segments as high risk because of particular demographic factors or favor others. This can be harmful in critical areas such as consumer loans. Models are reviewed regularly and data scientists are able to make adjustments.

Privacy Concerns: We have traded our privacy to gain more convenience. You can argue that apps which use AI know parts of our lives, maybe even more intimately than we know ourselves. Driving history, for example. AI systems require large amounts of data, raising concerns about how personal data is collected, stored, and used. Regulators have provided guidance, and misuse is levied penalties.

Transparency: AI models, especially deep learning models, can be complex and difficult to interpret, making it hard to understand how they make decisions. Even tinkering with logistic regression alone, which is a less complicated machine learning tool, made me feel I had less direct influence on my ability to manage variables, unless advised by my data experts. Determining who is accountable for the actions and decisions made by AI systems can be challenging.

Security Risks: AI systems may be vulnerable to cyberattacks, like other existing technology systems. But what is disconcerting is that it is being used for malicious purposes, including creating deep fakes. You must have already read about a company losing $25 million when an employee was fooled into thinking that it was the boss who made the instruction (Toubson, 2024).

Job Displacement: AI has the potential to automate many jobs, leading to job displacement and economic disruption for certain sectors and individuals. The key solution here is the need for programs to help workers move up to higher-value roles and develop skills that take advantage of AI technologies.

Environmental Impact and Power Usage: The training of large AI models requires significant computational resources, leading to high electricity consumption and significant environmental impact. I think this can be managed as long as companies are aware and make decisions balancing usage and sustainability considerations.

I can't even begin writing about philosophical and existential issues related to AI ethics, which are legitimate but partially influenced by Hollywood movies. I am leaving this to the experts.

What gives me comfort is that these issues are being raised and discussed in many forums. There will be initial overreaction brought about by uncertainty but, over time, we will find an acceptable way forward because AI is simply massively compelling.

Finally, a recent experience convinced me that certain human skills are still hard to replace. The heavy traffic in the Golden Horn area in Istanbul was brutal, and my app suggested it was a hopeless case, advising we should be ready to walk hundreds of meters to our small hotel. Lo and behold, in a couple of minutes, by some stroke of genius and after expressing his desperation, the driver weaved through the maze and got us almost right to the doorstep, where I met Osmanthesecurity. (There's more about Osman in Chapter Eleven.) Human creativity is still capable of surprises.

Living with AI

The banking sector is undergoing significant transformation. In particular, the rise of AI has the capability to automate and even eliminate many routine tasks.

The interesting irony is that, as AI continues to evolve, the value of personal banking and personalized services is becoming more relevant. Maybe it is helped by the rising number of senior citizens. Rather than rendering personal bankers obsolete, AI is now beginning to be harnessed to augment banker capabilities, thereby enhancing the customer experience.

This reminds me of a phase in fashion revolution. While RTW or ready-to-wear became the 'in' thing, it actually made bespoke and handmade less common, and consequently, more valuable. We don't hear the RTW term now, probably because those fashion houses wanted to drop the impersonal image. Will the same thing happen to digital banking?

Digital banking has radically changed how customers manage their finances, doing it anywhere where there is a signal. Despite the newfound convenience, the human element in banking remains irreplaceable. Personal bankers play a crucial role in understanding individual customer needs and building trusting relationships.

Thankfully, there is a wonderful compromise. AI, at least in my bank, is not viewed as a replacement for bankers, but as a powerful tool to enhance their effectiveness. By automating routine tasks and giving curated real-time data and insights, AI frees up personal bankers to focus on more complex services.

The potential for a higher level of personalization can lead to deeper relationships and enhance the quality of face-to-face meetings. People value empathy, understanding, and trust. Personal bankers can use AI to enhance these interactions by being better prepared and more knowledgeable about their clients' financial situations.

The filing clerks were not massacred; they learned computer skills, had productive lives, and are probably retired happily watching Netflix. When skills are threatened by obsolescence, humans adjust by learning that job-killer skill, and bring along their knowledge of their work/domains, customer relationships and ability to work with colleagues, all of which continue to be substantially useful.

Leaders have the obligation to anticipate the future, provide upskilling opportunities, and acquire the new technology. This way, both the workforce and the company can reinvent themselves and outperform others.

This combination of technology and human touch will provide the winning edge in the digital future. It can create a superior customer experience that digital-only platforms may never be able to replicate. Only time will tell.

GenAI and Cultural Transformation

The bank has always been a believer in AI, with over 50 machine learning (ML) models across products, excluding those AI tools we subscribed to for control functions.

Lately, we have been approached by external companies that use AI for credit scoring, although the jury is still out on most of those as the interest rates charged are way higher than what I would be comfortable quoting our customers. High rates also tend to adverse-select (jargon for saying only desperate borrowers would pay beyond 5% per month). Just the same, I am still impressed by the developments made in this area.

My preference has always been to monetize AI, and this is more apparent in using it to augment the productivity of our salespeople. Our machine learning models have been focused primarily on sales activity, leads generation in particular.

Recently, we launched a project on Generative AI, to reinforce ML. The results are very encouraging. For example, as we use our best salespeople to train or develop the new models, somehow the DNA of our superstars become part of how our new recruits learn the trade.

I never thought of GenAI as a cultural tool, but it is happening before my eyes.

Truly, AI makes the workforce more intelligent.

AI for Good

AI did not just appear out of nowhere. It is the latest in a long line of inventions that humanity has created to make living more efficient and meaningful. From the time cavemen carved stones into sharp edges, discovered fire, drew on walls, spoke rudimentary languages, and learned to live in harmony, each invention has been a step toward improving our way of life.

More recently, we have witnessed the evolution of technology through telex machines in my youth, calculators in my college days, computers when I started working as a banker, and the software that accompanied them. These innovations made us faster, more efficient, and enabled us to quickly make sense of the world around us, thus enhancing our productivity.

However, as the world evolved, so did our problems. AI emerged at a crucial time when we needed to ensure that dirty money did not infiltrate our banks, perpetuate pedophilia, and other crimes. AI allows us to instantaneously sweep through voluminous data, identify patterns of illicit activity, and even predict high-risk accounts. Without AI, we would be helpless in the face of such complex challenges.

Imagine a world without AI. We would struggle to manage the vast amounts of data generated every minute, every day. The efficiency and speed that we have come to rely on would diminish, leaving us vulnerable. The wildly complex web of global transactions would become impossible to monitor.

Even as we acknowledge the indispensable role of AI, it is essential to remain hopeful. AI is not just a tool for efficiency; it represents the most recent development in a long chain that exemplifies the collective pursuit of progress that defines humanity. Every time a new challenge arises, we find innovative solutions, driven by our desire to create a better world. It serves as a reminder that we must use this powerful technology responsibly.

Virtual Vogue: 'GQ' Meets AI

I've decided, after turning 60, to mine my closet for old clothes to mix with my new ones. But figuring out what goes well with what has always been perplexing to a provincial guy like me. At one point in my life, after PNB, I only had 5 days' worth of casual clothes. It was like I was ready only for 2-day weekends. When I crossed over to UBP and business casual became in, my wardrobe naturally expanded.

From a statistical standpoint, the question is: how many mixes can you create using your existing clothes? This concept, known as Combinations, has a formula. Unfortunately, colors, textures, and seasons add constraints. Not all colors go well together.

You can maximize the combinations by having more neutrals: khaki/beige pants, navy blue pants, dark olive green pants, dark blue shirt, white shirt, light blue shirt, navy blazer, cream blazer, blue and white striped shirt, and a few more in the list like black and gray.

The statistical formula for combinations works for these neutrals, and you can add one colorful item for accent. Outside of this list, it's hard to put everything together without looking like a fruit salad, which is better eaten than worn.

In the past, I would turn to Google and check images for inspiration. But nothing works better than AI. Using AI apps, you can ask what shirt goes well with which pants and blazers, and even shoes. AI becomes your style consultant, considering not only the colors and patterns but also the latest trends and personal preferences. It's like having a personal stylist who knows your closet inside out.

These digital consultants can suggest outfits for different occasions, predict weather-appropriate attire, and ensure that your combinations are always on point. Embracing technology in fashion allows you to maximize your wardrobe without constantly buying new items. It's smart, efficient, and stylish—a perfect blend of fashion and function.

Three Things I Learned from Prof. Chris

Physicists were celebrating when we found out that John Hopfield and Geoffrey Hinton won the Physics Nobel Prize for discoveries that paved the way for the development of artificial intelligence. Coincidentally, it was the same day we had Dr. Christopher Monterola over to give senior management a lecture on AI.

Chris, a physics PhD who used to teach at UP Diliman, has long been immersed in machine learning and the latest advancements in AI. He is currently the head of AIM's Aboitiz School of Innovation, Technology, and Entrepreneurship. Before this, he worked with the Singapore government's tech think tank for many years.

The session was enlightening, and I jotted down three main takeaways to bring back to the office:

1. The Power of Information

The information we put out on the web feeds into what Generative AI scans. When customers start asking their favorite AI apps, those apps will go through our website, the news, and everything else we publish. This underscores the importance of maintaining accurate and relevant online content.

2. Motivating the Team

Chris emphasized the importance of motivating the team and giving them the confidence to code and learn AI skills by picking three projects they can win. Early successes will fuel more experimentation and enthusiasm. Interestingly, these projects don't have to be directly related to their bank roles; instead, they should align with their passions.

3. AI Improvements

AI is getting better. The incidence of "hallucination"—instances where AI generates incorrect or nonsensical information—will drop significantly over time. In a few years, AI's hallucination rate is predicted to be below human levels, reducing the rate of errors and misinformation.

Additionally, Chris provided insights on affluence migration, highlighting trends on where deposits are moving over time. He also reminded us to continually track our company's digital maturity level to stay ahead in the rapidly evolving tech landscape.

To top it all off, Chris showcased an old interview of mine, translating it into French and half a dozen other languages. The audience was wowed, but the most impressive part for me was hearing myself speak Tagalog. Coming from the south, my Tagalog isn't the best, so that was a delightful surprise!

In essence, the lecture was a treasure trove of insights and practical advice. I walked away not just with a better understanding of AI, but also with actionable steps to bring these learnings to life in our organization.

"

Unlearning and relearning give a much more resounding AHA compared to learning for the first time.

Chapter Eight

Lifelong Learning

The last time I tinkered with Excel spreadsheets and charts was two decades ago when I headed regional derivatives sales and structuring for Citi, based in Singapore. Imagine my discomfort when our first lesson in Statistics and Data Analysis required data visualization through pivot tables.

I have been spoiled by my brilliant assistants, who did the dirty work for me in the last two decades. I did Excel "verbally." So I practiced and practiced, and did my homework, hoping the skills would become intuitive again.

Invest in Yourself

I remember a newspaper used to call me annually for a poll on investment strategies. There was a year when I was a heavy supporter of Australian dollars, for example. But, every year, I would persuade the readers to invest in themselves, learn new skills.

Whether you agree or not, bachelor's degrees and even graduate degrees do not completely prepare you for jobs. Such was my case.

Even if grad school qualified me from being a physicist to someone eligible for management jobs, banking was still far different. It took another 4 months for Citi to make a junior banker out of me. That wasn't enough. I was soon off to the 1-month Operations in Banking course with executive trainees from Hong Kong to India.

Every year, we would be sent to at least 1-week-long workshop on product, credit, or selling skills. This was often held in Singapore, until the training center was moved back to Manila.

We would compare notes with our colleagues on which courses were better and relevant. Our classmates were our peers from around Asia.

When assigned to a department, there were function-specific programs that were taken to qualify bankers for senior tasks. I remember doing four risk management seminars, the last one being in New York, which would have qualified me to be a senior risk officer. It was that methodical and thorough.

In the 90s, there was rapid advancement in derivative products. Luckily, I was chosen to specialize in the field. Hence, I had three times as much training together with a dozen representatives from Asian countries to get us up the curve fast. Later on, as the understudy of the country head, I was made to attend courses so I could learn other banking functions in-depth.

Indeed, training was the primary way to enhance human capital. In our industry, where competition is based on skills, such investment is crucial. I still subscribe to this process; hence, in our bank, we invest heavily in training. Branch operations might be the most structured of all the groups, with training at every level. We also run several types of management training programs. Nowadays, there is extra emphasis on digital skills.

With the abundance of knowledge resources internally and externally, all it takes for any individual is initiative. Surely, there is guidance from supervisors, but a self-driven junior can quickly advance. Young people are also going back to school. There is significant demand for graduate programs in data science, analytics, fintech, cybersecurity, and innovation.

I have seen evidence that among young bankers, there is a stronger motivation to better themselves. With AI and analytics making some jobs less relevant while augmenting others, it is mandatory for any ambitious young officer to learn new skills. Otherwise, he or she will be left behind.

The Enthusiastic Student

Forty years ago, it was about scoring points during class participation. Maybe the professors at that time encouraged such behavior, or maybe, it was just me and a number of equally competitive classmates. There was my finance professor who called on me three times every session. Unfortunately, that put me on the firing line, as I had to defend my presentation. The opposite extreme was the corporate finance professor, who would ignore me until the last 5 minutes when he would ask me to close the case.

The pressure to perform initially came from having to maintain my scholarship. What sustained me was the urge to keep learning from subjects I knew little about. I was one of the most ignorant at the start as many of my classmates were either business majors or already had 3 years of work experience.

In my 2 months at HBS 10 years ago, I took a back seat during our small group discussions and started to comment only midway. I must have overdone it because they complained I was no longer active. Somehow, I found the right balance afterward. In class, I was back to my energetic self. The professors encouraged discussion and debate in a class of 180 C-suite executives. When groupthink emerged, they identified a handful of participants to argue opposing, unpopular points. I remember those 2 months fondly.

Now, with a group of experienced classmates in our DBA class, I am thoroughly satisfied leaning back and absorbing the flow without the pressing need to recite. And when I raise my hand two or three times a session, it is because of an "aha" moment—when I realize something new that I can't wait to share. I have those moments even in statistics; I kid you not.

Having a wonderful and diverse mix of backgrounds (we have nine CEOs and country heads) across various industries is very powerful. I learn from everyone, and I always feel enriched each time I leave the class. I make extra notes about what I should start applying at work or write about.

School Grades and Becoming a Better Man

For the first time since 1987, I was staring at my school grades. I took my time, relishing the feeling of accomplishment, and more importantly, the immense relief. I started laughing, shaking my head.

CEOs are not supposed to go back to formal school. My study habits have remained intact, even if my retention capacity has seen better days. Too many memories stored—maybe I should complain. But these memories and experiences are exactly what make the incremental, even radical, learning so massively satisfying. Unlearning and relearning give a much more resounding "AHA" compared to learning for the first time.

I still pay attention to my scores, of course. They tell me if I missed anything. For example, I was so engrossed with one part of a paper that I missed a critical portion. My professor pointed that out in his remarks, and that was a lesson well learned. Another time, I started miserably in an exam. I recovered by starting from the last question, working my way backward.

I study hard, but I don't kick myself for getting things wrong in exams. Instead, I find out where I made mistakes, and I feel better knowing what the answer should have been. And doing the latter makes me, well, complete. Contrast that to decades ago when I agonized over each point.

When you realize you have been doing something wrong all along, when you accept that there are better ways to look at issues, and when you discover other points of view that you never knew existed, then you become a better man (or woman).

Maybe it is because I have little left to prove. Maybe it is because I am old enough to know that learning, by itself is the goal—not grades. Maybe it is because using my newfound knowledge to change things at work and improve my writing has spiced up my days. Maybe I have finally understood what wisdom really means.

The CEO's 2025 Lesson Plan

Being a CEO is much more difficult nowadays. I swear it was easier a decade ago. Now, there are new challenges to face and higher expectations to meet than ever before.

1. Diversity and Inclusion: It is not enough to hire leaders and employees from various backgrounds. You also need to include them in the way you run your business, and when possible, turn diversity into a source of better decisions and strategies.

2. Data and AI: If data are the new oil, you better start drilling by hiring quants and acquiring analytical tools while protecting data privacy and instilling data governance. A strategy on how to automate jobs and augment capabilities using AI is now mandatory.

3. Digitalization and Cybersecurity: Cyber risk has grown exponentially as you digitally transform your organization. Business models are evolving, and new entrants can steal your business if you don't pivot fast enough.

4. Work from Home (WFH): You may need to compromise with a hybrid arrangement as employees also look for social interactions to balance the time being saved from long commutes or heavy traffic and the comfort or convenience of being at home. Be prepared to trade control for trust.

5. Sustainability: Regulators now require an annual report on sustainability efforts, while there are investor groups who are wary of companies that "greenwash" their reports.

6. Inflation: With reverse globalization, disruption of supply chains, fiscal deficits, and defense spending, interest rates are bound to stay higher than historical levels. Be ready.

7. Cultural Transformation: All of the above will demand an organization that is agile, resilient, and collaborative. You need to accelerate the

change. All these will require leaders who can lead teams that lead the change.

What makes it difficult, but not impossible, also makes it worthwhile. After all, if it were easy, everyone would be doing it. Embrace the chaos, because that's where the magic happens. And remember, a little humor and a lot of coffee can go a long way in navigating the complexities of modern leadership.

Past Imperfect

Back in the early 80's, as a physics undergrad at the University of San Carlos, academic excellence was one of my top priorities. I was a scholar, and there was a minimum average to satisfy. I was diligent with my homework, enough to do well on my tests. However, I didn't go the extra mile by solving additional sample problems or seeking past tests from seniors. I needed time for student organizations.

I realized that putting in double the effort could substantially raise my marks. I sometimes invested the extra time when it seemed worthwhile. I was not philosophical enough to declare that mistakes were part of the journey, but I always made sure to identify where I went wrong and learn from those errors. This approach, I felt, was more efficient than just doubling my efforts. The goal was always to understand the lessons better, even if mistakes initially brought some disappointment.

Decades later, now that I am back in school for my DBA and actively involved in business transformation, my approach has evolved. While I continue to be diligent, I have become much more accepting of my mistakes, as long as I make an earnest effort to get them right next time.

This shift in perspective has made learning more enjoyable. In the bank and in other companies, there is a word for this: agile. We keep improving our offerings even if they are imperfect, and we promptly address customer problems and complaints, using them to further innovate our products. Agile is more efficient, although there are times when, due to regulatory reasons, we try to reduce errors to the barest minimum.

Ultimately, the process of learning and growing through my mistakes has taught me that perfection is an illusion. In the agile method, I am not even sure what is ideal, but we keep moving toward it until, somehow, we come close to perfection.

Should You Take Your MBA?

It is quite common to see young professionals going back to school for their master's degrees, or completing certification programs, even if there is an ongoing debate as to the relevance of an MBA. Meanwhile, there continues to be demand for the course as schools have made great efforts to reinforce programs, making them more relevant in terms of content and delivery.

An MBA program is appropriate for those who have never had management preparation during their undergraduate studies and are aspiring for management careers.

As a physics major in the 80's, I was a perfect example of someone hopelessly clueless about marketing, finance, and operations. I learned accounting from an introductory book a month before classes began. I needed an MBA as I wanted to enter the business world equipped with the required knowledge.

Most STEM graduates, except maybe Industrial Engineering majors, are good candidates. And I will hasten to add that I believe business administration, industrial/management engineering majors, and the like are wasting their time and money doing MBAs. In fact, I persuade them to take more specialized courses instead of doing an expensive review.

However, and this is a huge "however," not all business undergrad courses, just like not all MBA programs, are created equal.

This brings me to my second point. What I would like to suggest is that young professionals upgrade their skills by taking the next course at a school with proven expertise/rating in the field, one that employs a different teaching method, like the case study (versus the generally lecture-type style in undergrad), or one whose curriculum has subjects unfamiliar to the potential student, with expert professors teaching those subjects. Finally, and this is a crucial point, student diversity is designed to reinforce learning, as it enriches class discussions. (This is one of the main reasons I enjoy my DBA class.)

The answer may not even be graduate school. More and more, I see professional certifications in technical or digital fields like cybersecurity, risk management, and sustainability. If you browse LinkedIn, you will notice many profiles with a string of letters following their names. (Fahrenheits, as I call them, inspired by *Don't Stop Me Now* (Mercury, 1978), a song by the Queen.)

Every potential master's student, or anyone pursuing advanced courses, has to make this determination. In addition to gathering info, they should consult their mentors and seniors who have gone through the process before.

Let me share what I did. I enrolled for my advanced degrees while taking professional certifications over time. They were relevant to my role at that point, allowing me to apply new knowledge immediately. I learned from school, from online courses, and on the job.

If I had to do it all over again, I would do non-business (maybe physics/computer science or behavioral science or both), then take my MBA.

Been Framed

One morning, at 3:00 AM Europe time, I woke up early to attend a 9:00 AM class, Manila time. I was not going to miss this, despite the short sleep, especially because I found the materials interesting and thought-provoking. Prof. Jammu Francisco structured the discussion around a specific framework that, while it had its critics, it also had a significant following among practitioners and academicians. This framework was the Resource-Based View (RBV). Maybe because I finished grad school in the 80's, I had never heard of it, not even during my 2 months in Boston a decade ago. Instead, I thrived on Porter's competitive framework and the popular SWOT analysis.

Business is not physics. Frameworks are not theories, but they serve as an excellent guide—a checklist, if you will—and help start discussions with others familiar with the concepts. It is like a sub-language. These frameworks simplify complex concepts and allow for structured thinking. They provide a common ground for dialogue and collaboration, enabling practitioners to systematically dissect and tackle business problems.

This realization got me thinking. I had actually written some frameworks that I used when mentoring or plotting strategy. However, I am well aware of the fallibility of my formulations. This was, in fact, one reason why I enrolled in the DBA program. I needed to figure out some theoretical or empirical basis for what I had been proposing.

My academic pursuit is not just about gaining credentials but about integrating practical wisdom with insights. It is about bridging the gap between practice and theory, ensuring that my frameworks are not just intuitively sound but also academically rigorous.

Reflecting on this journey, I realized that frameworks, whether self-devised or academically endorsed, are invaluable tools. Yet, frameworks must be validated against real-world scenarios and academic research to truly serve their purpose.

One Senior Life

When you go back to study again, you don't get the equivalent of a senior discount. You have to work as hard as the younger kids. You want the opportunity; be careful what you wish for. But the best part is that I can truly say that I am doing this purely for the joy of learning.

Of course, I need to pass the assessments, group work, and homework assigned. I figured out how to do this efficiently by re-reading the slides and redoing exercises by myself after class. This process hammers the concepts deep into my skull.

Almost four decades ago, I learned Expected Value in quantitative analysis over a couple of classes and cases. This time, it was simply inserted into probability theory like a "by the way" comment: explained in 10 minutes. Excel-assisted learning has really accelerated calculations. But the point is not the calculation tools; the point is to understand when to use which analytics tools and why.

We learn by doing. We relearn by sharing, by collaborating. And unlearn and learn even more when we correct our mistakes.

I have also benefited from my experience and those of my classmates. In our Grand Challenges class, Prof. Felipe Calderon has posed a most interesting set of management journal articles. Our task is to understand the research methodology, highlight if it is unique, and derive insights from the materials.

Work experience and "general wisdom" from my last almost four decades provide a baseline. When I add up the experiences of my classmates and professor, it amounts to 600 years. Six hundred!

Yeah, but therein lies a numerical fallacy. Adding up assumes we have mutually exclusive pasts, which isn't the case at all. We have common experiences—in similar jobs and the same decades. Therefore, we need to make a huge adjustment. We have to deduct the "experience intersection," which probably adds up to more than half the original total.

Still, that will be at least over two centuries of wisdom.

Learning from Home

I had new thoughts about WFH when I started attending DBA sessions live in school.

In class, when the subject matter is new and difficult, you can always ask your seatmate. Or you can compare your workbooks. A single misstep can easily be checked. This was helpful when I was relearning data visualization using Excel. The young ones were faster than the "young once".

During coffee breaks, there is more time for interaction and sharing of insights. What you may have missed, you can clarify. Then, there is the added benefit of banter and cajoling, which builds rapport and engagement. And bonding.

Compare this to learning by Zoom, where class interaction is hard. Let's not even consider distractions. When we take this one step further, by learning through recorded videos, most of the dynamics are missed.

I recall spending days in a physical class when taking my British Computer Society UX Foundation Certificate. That was the toughest exam I ever took, and I believe that physical presence made a difference. The MIT and Oxford certifications were mostly recorded lessons, but with optional remote live lectures and plenty of group work and meetings supervised by teaching assistants. The subjects—AI, Blockchain, and Fintech—had novelty 6 years ago, so there was motivation to learn.

I believe that learning demands at least two things: first, that the student meets the standard or maximizes the transfer of knowledge and skills, and second, that the student remains engaged and eager to keep going.

Weekly get-togethers in hybrid work arrangements are a good compromise, but only if employees are already adequately trained or are highly skilled. What concerns me is that, in a number of cases, I am actually seeing higher employee turnover.

Why I Enrolled in the AIM DBA Program

I had been scanning doctorate programs for the last decade or so (admit it—you also did!), but I wasn't serious about it, especially because that was the time I switched employers. When initiating a growth-oriented business transformation, I needed to be completely focused. More energy is required when building momentum.

I last physically studied on campus 10 years ago when taking the Harvard Business School Advanced Management Program. The 200 cases over 8 weeks, plus another dozen professional certifications over the last 7 years, prepared me well for my present mission.

I completed my MBA 37 years ago. Now, I am back for my DBA as part of the first cohort of 18. This time, I am not the youngest in my class. This time, I am paying for my tuition fees.

The first few days were intense but collaborative, insightful, and inspiring. I credit it to the well-curated materials, world-class academic staff, and a wonderful mix of students. And yes, in true AIM style, we have a good contingent of foreigners (although all have strong links to the country).

Why study again?

First, while writing my two books and over 200 LinkedIn posts, I found myself researching concepts. My method consisted of writing a draft, then checking possible theoretical basis or contrary ideas before posting. While my musings never appeared academic, my process exposed me to academic articles. I started asking "why" very often. Over time, accepting practical methods or what I'd consider proven experience was no longer sufficient.

Second, I want to stay relevant in my senior years. There has been a rapid evolution in my favorite topics—digital transformation, sustainability, and inclusion—and I wish to continue to be a part of the discussions.

Finally, the force (to learn) continues to be strong with this one.

Who Should Pay for Training?

A reader posed an interesting question. She appreciated the training provided by her company but wished to do more to equip herself for her own future plans. She felt so strongly about it that she was willing to pay for it on her own. My instinctive answer was, "Go ahead!" This, to me, is a "good" problem because it highlights one of my concerns in training—employee aspiration.

There are three motivations at work here:

Company Requirements: The company needs to ensure employees are competent in their roles. Training ensures that they are. New tellers, for instance, do not sit at the counter without going through boot camp. Obviously, the company pays for this.

Regulatory Requirements: For specific jobs, regulators require some level of minimum qualifications before the professional is allowed to interact with the public at large. The company is mandated to take care of this.

Employee Aspirations: Employees may wish to qualify for future jobs and invest in themselves beyond what is currently required. This is where it is unclear who pays. There are companies that truly invest in a high-potential employee's future through scholarships.

However, not all companies have the resources or policies to fund additional training. In such cases, employees often find themselves in a dilemma. Should they invest their own money into further training, hoping that it will pay off in their current role or future opportunities?

A practical approach would be for the employee to present a proposal to their superiors. Demonstrating how the new skills will directly contribute to the company's objectives can make a compelling case for shared investment in training. Ultimately, it's about creating a culture where continuous learning is valued and supported.

Part Three

Gaining Gravitas,
Channeling Charm

"

Balancing strengths with the conscious effort to improve weaknesses makes us versatile.

Chapter Nine

Word of Mouth

In my last keynote, I exclaimed, "It is so much fun here!" At another event held on an island resort, I told the crowd I was inspired to write a post entitled "Son of a Beach." Both were authentic as they were unplanned, funny, and sincere.

However, these comments need to be relevant to the topic and not off-context. That is why I avoid starting a speech with a quote from a dead person. I find it unnatural. I would rather quote one of the previous speakers if they said something insightful or intriguing.

Getting to 36K Followers in 12 Months

After I started to write actively on LinkedIn on October 27, 2023, I soon got in touch with my buddy, Eric Sim, who has an amazing almost 3 million followers. He had a simple formula: content, consistency, and community. I followed it to the letter.

I posted content that was compelling, like issues on bad bosses, difficult subordinates, and people paid higher salaries. I also tried to address current issues while avoiding controversial ones (no politics, no vaccines, and no religion) and topics that were contentious. I kept a long list of possible topics in my iPhone notes.

Where did I obtain my content? Well, I am naturally curious. I researched topics I did not know much about, like the life expectancy of CEOs. It also helped that I had competency in various topics; old age has its benefits.

I did this consistently by composing every weekend, putting out up to three posts, mostly on Sundays, and completing a few more during the week. Since I don't play golf and am generally a homebody, I had time for this.

I Googled the best time for posting. The advice was Tuesday to Thursday, 8:00 AM to 10:00 AM, and around lunchtime. The truth is, I never followed it. I found that the absolute best time to post was in the afternoon of the last day of a 3-day holiday. I hit over a thousand likes multiple times by doing this.

Community was a multiplier. Eric put me in his community, and I benefited from his endorsement. I linked up with new connections. When I wrote about Citibank, I had old colleagues coming out from everywhere. My posts on data science connected me to their community. And I started accepting invitations to conferences and other complementary activities like podcasts. Eric was right (of course!)—my follower rate jumped to two to four times the usual daily rate.

Finally, I think the conversational tone was crucial, including crafting the language to make it clear, simple, and cheerful. It reads like I'm talking.

Becoming an Author

Ever since I was a kid, I enjoyed reading books on pretty much everything. Writing was not among my favorite activities. In fact, composing theme reports was a chore I disliked. Why did they always ask us what I did during my summer vacation? Maybe the problem had to do with the subject matter. Somehow, we never wrote about "why anything."

I broke into the writing scene in grade six by winning an essay competition on a Christmas topic. Nothing much else followed thereafter.

All those years, I kept reading, and later on, when I had some money, I started buying books regularly. I was keen on novels by Frederick Forsyth, but after college, I switched almost entirely to non-fiction. Books by management gurus were the "in" thing then, different from the more behavioral themes nowadays.

I started writing on Facebook in 2009, with only a few sentences each post. This went on for 14 years. I developed a writing style that my first book editor thought was uniquely mine. You see, I write the way I speak. It is conversational rather than formal business English. So, you could say my writing was meant to record my talks. It was during my first year as a CEO that I had more practice doing long pieces. I preferred writing my own speeches because reading somebody else's work felt unnatural. The more talks I did, the more speeches I collected. They formed the second half of my first book, *Never Stand Alone*.

Deciding to release my memoir in time for my 60th birthday got me writing for 19 days, filling up the first hundred pages of book one. What I did not anticipate was that the momentum would carry me through to books two and three.

I write because it relieves stress; it's a form of release. I write because I have thoughts in my head that I want to record; otherwise, I will forget them. And I write because I was inspired by the authors whose works I have admired through the decades.

A Personal Brand

There was a corporate trainer in the 90s who lectured about personal branding during a leadership workshop. I was a bit of a rebel back then and did not accept new concepts unless convinced. I frankly thought it was a terrible waste of time and that he was just introducing a new gimmick.

I changed my views on the topic later on. I found it had some merit, but mostly because it was a reminder to exercise caution. Why? Because it leads to people being too liberal in labeling themselves with certain phrases like "strategic thinkers", "global connectors", "visionaries", "innovators", and even without a payroll, calling themselves "CEOs".

We have to avoid superficial portrayal of one's abilities because people can actually tell the difference. Many individuals adopt lofty terms without being worthy of the qualities and experience they describe. This disconnect and dishonesty can erode trust. And it is unfair to the real, deserving experts.

On the day my first book made it to the local bestseller list after 3 months of good sales, I thought of putting the word "bestseller" in my LinkedIn profile, laughed many times about it. I did not want to tempt fate, and destroy the chances of my second book. There are established bestsellers in the country, while I am an amateur.

I am still writing because it makes me happy. It gives me happy hormones and reduces my stress. This enthusiasm has led to my accepting invitations to external events, and I have become a keen public speaker as well.

In the end, my personal brand is not how I describe myself. It is about what I write, how the readers feel when they read my work, how it entertains them, and how it helps them think differently about their careers, their lives, and the world around them.

I write for "haha" and "aha!" moments. When you have either one, or better yet both of these, then I have made a connection.

From Terrified to Terrific

I believe that most of so-called strengths are built early in life by teachers and arbiters who identify potential performers based on physical traits, class honors, or even gregariousness as a proxy for elocution/drama. They focus their energy on the chosen few, while giving token effort on the vast majority.

The consequence for the unfortunate majority is that innate talent can end up latent, enveloped in a lack of confidence, and only when lucky or left with no choice, discovered later in life. Late bloomers could have been early bloomers if not for the figurative roll of the dice in school.

It is a Darwinian story of the fittest thriving initially, but ultimately won by those who adapt and find the confidence to reach deep into their being to become better versions of themselves.

When I was a kid, I was one of the smallest in class—a biological consequence of being younger than most and a weakling who couldn't run middle distances. I would have had a better chance if I entered school a year later. Fast forward to my forties, I completed several 10k runs and could do 21k. This transformation wasn't just about building stamina but overcoming a lifelong artificial weakness resulting from a kindergarten entry decision.

Public speaking used to terrify me. The thought of standing in front of an audience made my hands shake and my voice tremble. Yet, by facing this fear head-on, I became a frequently invited keynote speaker, delivering speeches to thousands. The journey from fear to confidence in public speaking wasn't hard once I overcame my self-doubt. This happened in fourth-year high school when, believe it or not, I volunteered to represent my class in a school-wide contest. It felt reckless but I came in second.

As an aspiring editor, my early attempts were sloppy at best. I realized that what I enjoyed was writing rather than running the paper. To be honest, feature writing was not a strength of my school, which preferred the sciences and technical education. However, persistence paid off. I went on to publish two books, turning a former weakness into a personal accomplishment.

These experiences taught me that focusing solely on strengths can be limiting. By embracing and working on my weaknesses, I discovered the potential for remarkable growth. From a statistical standpoint, addressing weaknesses can be transformative. Imagine a pie chart of skills and abilities. By focusing only on the largest segments, you ignore the opportunity to develop the smaller ones. When you put effort into those weaker areas, the entire pie expands, giving you a more balanced skill set.

Balancing strengths with the conscious effort to improve weaknesses makes us versatile. This balance prepares us for a wider array of challenges and opportunities.

Getting into the Rhythm

People have routines they follow when preparing for special events that require them to be at their best. These are developed over time, maybe even with a bit of superstition. Some bring props, while others have special requests. What matters is that these seem to work, and following the process helps boost confidence.

When I am set to address a large audience, I follow the following steps, almost without fail.

First, I prepare my script weeks in advance so I have time to rewrite it at least twice. The first draft contains the general idea. The second adds some literary flair. Going through the rewrites also helps me internalize the speech, allowing me to deliver it without reading from the script.

Second, I design how the slides should look to support my message. They should be simple, uncluttered, and easy to absorb so the audience will focus on me, not the slides, the vast majority of the time.

Third, I read the words aloud, checking if they sound right. I ask myself: *Should I change some phrases? When do I speak slowly or quickly? When do I stress for impact? And where are the pregnant pauses?*

Fourth, I make sure my assistant knows when to flip the slide. I usually stay away from the clicker as much as possible. It distracts me from my message.

Fifth, I sleep well the night before and eat half a meal to avoid any discomfort.

Finally, when I am at the podium, I smile and scan the crowd. By the way, I almost never start or end my speech with a quote from some wise person. Instead, I make a remark inspired by who or what I see in the crowd.

The objective is to win the crowd early, draw them away from their phones, and convey the main messages in an engaging and entertaining way.

Talk of the Town: Juggling Multiple Speeches

I used to accept only one or two long speeches monthly. My day job made it difficult to accept more, although my position is also the reason I get invited. Anything 20 minutes or longer demands extra preparation; I need to deliver a quality that gives me personal satisfaction. Lately, the invitations have multiplied. My hobby—writing—is to blame. Fortunately, it is also because of writing that I am able to accept more.

The secret is content. I have plenty of it from my two books and almost 14 months of LinkedIn posts. For example, my opening keynote during the Philippine Mentoring Summit was based on the second chapter, *Find a Jedi Master*, from my second book, *Reinvent and Outperform: Becoming a Better Leader*.

Still, I need to manage three limiting constraints:

1. Sleep: I shouldn't sleep less than my usual 8 hours for more than two consecutive days.

2. Voice: I should take care of my voice to prevent strain.

3. Adrenaline: I should monitor my excitement level to avoid adrenaline fatigue after events.

Each one is a showstopper. I can manage the first two, but the third one is becoming increasingly difficult.

How do I scale speaking?

1. Modular Materials: My materials are like Lego pieces on specific subtopics, which reduce preparation time. I customize only a portion of the slides for new audiences.

2. Pace Myself: I spread out my schedule to avoid back-to-back speeches on different topics, especially new ones. Repeating topics can be less draining and allows for relaxation. I accept some boredom for the sake of efficiency.

3. Leverage GenAI: I use AI for background industry research, not for actual speeches, which I take time to write. A 20-minute piece consumes at least an hour and a half—often more.

4. Framework-Based Approach: I develop and use favorite frameworks based on common problems I encounter. Over time, this has streamlined my thinking process.

All these have made public speaking less of a chore for me, and I have begun to enjoy it more.

After a Speech, Adrenaline Dissipates

I write almost all my speeches (like all my LinkedIn posts), with only a few exceptions. I usually prepare well in advance for major events. The draft is finished weeks ahead of time, so there is time to rethink, recraft, and add the highlights. The build-up is not intense, as I take my time and do not cram.

For internal speeches in RCBC, I have the draft ready a week in advance. Sometimes, my assistants prepare talking points. Over the years, they've practiced writing following my style. Still, the ideas of my potential messages simmer in my head for weeks before I begin writing.

Then, I use several blank sheets of paper to describe the accompanying PowerPoint slides that will help stress the main points of my speech.

I am usually not tense or nervous anymore. I am just excited to let the show begin. This allows me to socialize a bit with other speakers and old friends. This is actually nice as it helps me compose a few ad-libs to personalize the speech further. I also listen to the speakers before me so I can help the organizers keep the theme consistent.

Otherwise, I cannot wait for my turn to stand on stage.

The problem arises after the performance. I get tired and want to sleep longer. Presentations are not physically demanding; they are more mentally taxing. But, somehow, it translates to physical exhaustion.

Maybe it has something to do with adrenaline build-up before the speech. I may sound relaxed, but deep inside, I'm already in the zone. My entire body conspires to make sure this old man does a decent job. When the talk is over, the extra burst of energy dissipates.

The best antidote is sleep, lots of it, so I hit the bed earlier than usual. Or a glass of Sauvignon Blanc. Or Riesling.

Anxiety on Live TV

Admittedly, going on live TV still makes me anxious, and my last half dozen interviews took a long time to prepare for. It was not just the content that mattered; I also needed time to psych myself up. Thankfully, that ended when I finally felt comfortable with this interview with Ron and Salve.

What changed? Well, three things.

First, my classmate Rico Camus gave me the best tip: focus on my interviewer and just have a conversation. I ignored the camera for the most part, except for the initial wide smile at the start. I do that during speeches, and I did it again this time.

Second, Ron Cruz had a chat with me before the show and told me he had read my first book (his wife has a copy) and that he follows me on LinkedIn. He assured me it was going to be a fun conversation.

And third, Salve Duplito already interviewed me before, so I was less nervous that time. We also see each other at financial advocacy and fintech events. I noticed that she made a lot of marks on her copy of my book, and we could have gone on for another hour. She is both a professional and personal friend.

It also helped that the topic was about my second book, something I obviously knew well. There were at least a dozen sound bites I could push, depending on where the conversation went. If they asked how I found time, I would say "I don't play golf". If they asked about my source of inspiration, I could mention my two boys and my mentees, and how Citibank had a strong mentorship culture.

But really, supportive colleagues and friends help me overcome hurdles. This goes beyond TV, as it applies to practically any activity requiring higher confidence. They make the process less daunting and more enjoyable. In the end, it wasn't just about being prepared. Overcoming my TV anxiety was a team effort.

Avoid Reading Your Slides

During external presentations, I generally ignore my slides and have someone flip them for me as I speak. Usually, this role is reserved for my assistant, who knows the script and topic well and helps me with the slides. Even if I ad-lib or skip parts, he knows which slides match my story. The funny downside is when he gets entertained by my unrehearsed jokes and forgets to press the next button.

My new favored style is to put one or two phrases on each slide, similar to what they do in TedX. This is quite neat because, after speed reading, the audience focuses their attention on me. It also doesn't take long to prepare the slides. Hurray!

I only refer to slides when numbers and tables are involved, especially during internal reports on business status. Still, using charts and other visual tools makes it easier to tell the story without pointing to details. This allows the audience to grasp the information intuitively and more quickly.

What I advise people to avoid is turning their slides into Word files. After all, I can read faster than they can talk. I usually don't criticize, as that would break their confidence, but I note it down as an opportunity to improve their skills. Yes, I have done this twice recently. I prefer to encourage their growth.

There was a time a month for me was quite a whirlwind. I had four long keynotes for large audiences, on topics ranging from advanced technology to mentoring; five short speeches for clients and colleagues; two business presentations; two book launches; and one TV interview. To manage all these, I needed to be more efficient.

My LinkedIn posts form most of my content. My assistant and I brainstorm and weave the materials into a cohesive narrative. It's a kind of Lego system that works well, helping me stay focused on my day job and making this busy schedule incredibly fulfilling.

Dissenting Opinion

Back in high school and college, teachers would sometimes encourage debate by writing an issue on the board and asking the class to state their opinions. One by one, classmates raised their hands, indicating their choice. I liked to choose last because I wanted to see how the class was divided. More often than not, the split was lopsided, with the easy side taken by most. By "easy," I mean the popular opinion.

I always took the unpopular stand as it was more challenging, and the stakes were far more attractive. There was no glory in winning an effortless position. And if you lose an unpopular stand, it is accepted to be a losing position anyway.

The popular position had known arguments and defenses. Their cards were on the table. This encouraged misguided confidence. On the other hand, the dissenting side had to come up with new, creative attack plans to discredit the majority. This was the exciting part.

There is an art to taking dissenting opinions. You can't be too identified as the one who always takes the opposite side just for fun, even if it is true. You cannot celebrate a win.

I remember attending a senior credit course with 40 other bankers in New York. During a case discussion, we were asked to decide whether to lend to a leading company in a high-risk sector. The tally was 38 against and 3 in favor. The three in favor were a young Latino, a Chinese senior credit officer, and the Hong Kong country treasurer. The latter took the side because he was convinced it was the right thing to do, and the majority opinion betrayed how bankers were supposed to act. To him, it was no longer just a case.

In the office setting, groupthink is dangerous. Decisions should not be based on popular opinion or what people think the boss wants. That just perpetuates the status quo. Instead, encourage free discussion, use of data, and willingness to be wrong. This will lead to new ideas, innovation, and new paths forward.

66

When a mentor witnesses their mentee eclipsing them, it's a moment of pride, not defeat.

Chapter Ten

Mentorship and Networking

I am grateful to the Philippine Society for Talent Development for inviting me to keynote the Philippine Mentoring Summit. Mentoring is more than just a project; it is a powerful way to accelerate the careers of the disadvantaged and help reduce social inequality in the country.

The junior bankers closest to me have been my three assistants, none of whom were raised in affluent urban settings. The first was half-orphaned, the son of an engineer who found work abroad, and was raised by his grandparents. The second comes from an island province, married her childhood sweetheart, and dedicates time to care for her widowed mother. The current one is from Central Luzon, whose father is a professor at a local college in their hometown.

They are a reminder of diverse paths that lead to success.

Career Lessons for Young Leaders

My mentees have made some realizations and surprising career moves and decisions. I am sharing the most surprising ones, anonymized:

1. You find out that you don't want what you're doing, so do what you want to do. He was always at the top of his class and graduated with flying colors. However, after graduation, he realized that the last 4 years had not been what he really wanted to do moving forward.

2. Find a workplace where you are valued. He was not getting support from his seniors, and his skills were being wasted on token jobs that did not add value to the company. He moved to another institution that embraced people with his background.

3. Find a new important skill to learn. She has always supported the finance team with her quantitative skills, found their work exciting, and made new friends. Now, she is pursuing her CFA certification to build new expertise.

4. Calibrate your ambition to reality. When you want to get far in life but lack resources and connections, you can still find alternative ways forward—even if it takes an extra year or two. You are still young. You can make it happen.

5. Family is a priority. When you find a job, current or new, that allows you to drive your kid to school or spend time with your young ones, choose that job.

6. A bit of pain is not bad, as long as you're learning. Companies are not perfect; they can have terrible shortcomings. I asked one mentee, "Is it worth the trouble?" She answered that she's still learning a lot. The discomfort is her tuition fee.

So far, so good.

It's a Small World, After All

Kevin Bacon has become a phenomenon for being one or two degrees away from anyone in Hollywood. His network is so expansive that, even if he does not know person X, he surely knows someone who can connect him to person X. I have found that concept interesting, together with Eric Sim's post on weak ties—those connections that open doors to new networks.

Since we move around the banking industry, Bacons are aplenty. Citibankers, Philnabankers, Unionbankers, CitySavingsBankers, and now RCBC bankers all tend to know almost everyone else. It helps spread messages, including new practices, bad borrowers, and the like. It also facilitates gossip, though, in most cases, it's untrue.

The problem with being too industry-focused is that we miss out on what's happening outside glass and concrete walls.

In the last 12 months, I have been gifted with new friendships beyond the banking and academic communities I belong to. As I look back, I realize that I made significant changes in my life and work habits, which have resulted in wonderful outcomes. They started as weak ties but have grown stronger since. Let me share a few:

First, my new classmates—my 18 new comrades—our teachers, and I, spend most of our Saturdays together, and some more hours doing group work. This has opened my mind to new viewpoints from experts in other specializations. Since these were focused discussions, you could say we bonded in the academic trenches.

Second, being active on LinkedIn gave me a platform to declare and express my views on various topics. I found like-minded folks of all ages with whom I exchange notes weekly. Sometimes, I get dissenting opinions, but we connect in the same way. I don't think I will meet most of them in person, but it's a new world anyway. At airports, I often bump into someone who follows me on LinkedIn.

Third, my mentees—40 of them—have been a source of joy and learning. I hope I have helped them with their careers and aspirations. We discussed their academic decisions, career switch plans, getting more acclimated in new environments, taking second chances, sharpening start-up strategies, and more. There was an unintended consequence: several of my articles stemmed from my exchanges with them, anonymized of course. This has allowed me to write not just from a personal viewpoint, but from a range of personal experiences. While not necessarily statistically significant, the consistency of these stories made them worthwhile to write about.

Finally, my two books have found readers who became acquaintances after they sent me their thoughts via FB, IG, or LinkedIn. I did not expect this much interaction. It felt good to find out that even people I did not know personally found the pages useful and entertaining.

As the kindergarten song goes, *it's a small world, after all* (Sherman & Sherman, 1964). It becomes one when you open your window, and reach out.

Belief in Human Decency

Over the years, I would randomly get a thank you note from someone I can no longer remember. They would mention an incident, sometimes decades ago, when I helped them and how much it mattered to them at that point.

I listened to them because there were times in my life when I felt lost, incompetent, or simply inadequate, and out of nowhere, someone would swoop in and lift me up. These individuals helped me for no reason other than human decency. Some strangers became friends in an instant, while others went on with their lives, telling me to not worry because "it was nothing." It was a big deal for me.

In high school, a neighbor stood guard against a bully who had made my misery his hobby. That small act showed me that people are willing to step up, even when they have no obligation to do so.

Then came my USC days. Since there were hardly any other physics majors, friends from other courses informally adopted me into their social circles. These groups became my allies, helping me navigate university life.

Fast forward to my time at UP, where I found a best friend who guided me through the complexities of being a faculty member in an unfamiliar environment.

At AIM, the kindness continued. The Admissions Director went above and beyond to secure my scholarship. One particular classmate even lent me a blazer for class events. These gestures made a world of difference. I haven't stopped thanking both of them.

Everywhere I went, I benefitted from acts of selflessness that have left a permanent mark on my life. If there's one thing I've learned, it's that kindness starts a chain reaction, the type that restores our faith in humanity.

When the Apprentice Eclipses the Master

I was staring at the beautiful painting *The Baptism of Christ* at the museum when I heard the legend of Andrea del Verrocchio, Leonardo da Vinci's mentor. As part of his apprenticeship, Leonardo painted an angel in Verrocchio's work. The angel was so beautifully executed that Verrocchio was said to have been so humbled that he decided to stop painting and focus on sculpture instead.

It's a fascinating story that highlights the dynamics between mentors and their students. As someone who has mentored many, I've seen my mentees flourish and achieve great things.

So, what is my view about this story? I will speak plainly and simply: I want my mentees to maximize their talent. I want them to be better than they were on their career paths before I met them. They stand on my shoulders and on the shoulders of other mentors, so they can see farther. My investment of time, knowledge, and experience is not to create replicas of myself but to empower others to improve themselves. If it results in surpassing my achievements, then I will be very proud and very happy.

Verrocchio's humility and acceptance of Leonardo's talent is a testament to true mentorship. It's not about competition; it's about fostering growth and potential. When a mentor witnesses their mentee eclipsing them, it's a moment of pride, not defeat.

For me, the ultimate success is seeing my mentees thrive, innovate, and make their own marks in the world. Their achievements reflect our collective effort and stand as a testament to the cycle of knowledge and learning.

So, here's to the apprentices who become masters, and to the mentors who celebrate their ascent. May we all aspire to lift others, knowing that their success is our greatest legacy.

A Mentor's Joy

You might say that a mentor's greatest joy is seeing their mentee succeed in their chosen career or find a partner and settle down. Those are good reasons.

Today, I found the best reason—and it has to do with the mentee helping build the careers of younger professionals when he becomes a mentor and teacher himself.

I first met Mykee Cruz about a decade ago. He was part of the famous Batch 5 of management trainees whose final interview round I witnessed. I later learned that he was raised by his grandparents after his mother died early and his father decided to work abroad. He joined his father in Singapore after high school (he was valedictorian) and worked for a good part of the year at KFC (he knows chicken). Then, he made it to the Ateneo de Manila University's Economics Honors Program.

I was on the lookout for new trainees to join my team and found him in corporate planning. He was soon attached to me and helped me run the thrift bank subsidiary that we acquired. We went through five acquisitions and traveled all over the islands until we both left to join RCBC.

As expected, he took his MBA, and again, as expected, he graduated with high honors.

He half-reluctantly moved to line management after his tour of duty as my special assistant, but thrived in his new role in digital banking. In fact, the skills he learned in his new position prepared him well for a secondary role—that of a fintech professor at our school.

Today, I saw him write about the last session of his class and how he prepared hard for it. His students responded with the most gracious compliments and expressions of gratitude.

As his mentor, I am beaming with pride. He went out of his comfort zone and followed my advice: *if it scares you, it is probably worth doing.*

Secret of Youth

I recently had the wonderful opportunity to chat with two young bankers, both bold and brilliant. Being quite close to their parents, I have been updated on their goings-on, including their love lives. My interest was to learn more about their current jobs and future plans. They are undeniably great raw material for future leadership positions because, even at a young age, they have impressed me immensely.

Later, I discovered that they were surprised by how generous I was with my time. That got me thinking deeply. Here's what I concluded:

Firstly, it feels like I am starting all over again by living vicariously through them. Having learned my lessons throughout my career, I realize that sharing my experiences with them gives them a better shot at success. Seeing them avoid the pitfalls I once stumbled upon and navigating their careers with informed decisions is incredibly fulfilling. It's like watching a better version of my younger self.

Secondly, sharing knowledge and experiences with them is a form of giving that never gets depleted. On the contrary, I find it recharging. Each conversation, each piece of advice, and every shared laugh fuels my own enthusiasm. It reminds me that the well of wisdom and experience isn't a finite resource. It grows and deepens with each exchange, making mentoring a rejuvenating experience.

Finally, these interactions offer me invaluable insights into the young talent within the bank. By engaging with them, I gain a clearer understanding of their motivations, aspirations, and the challenges they face. This perspective is crucial in cultivating an environment where young leaders can thrive.

In essence, my time with these young bankers isn't just about giving advice. It's a reciprocal relationship where I, too, gain knowledge, energy, and insights. It's a testament to the bottomless barrel of wisdom, where the more you give, the more you receive. And that, to me, is the essence of true leadership and growth.

Our Two-Speed Society: Education Is Not Enough

Sadly, experience has shown that education, while powerful, might not be enough as a social accelerator. The new, emerging middle class, propelled by degrees and some additional advantages, has widened the divide. It will take time before the rest of society can catch up.

I was encouraged to figure out ways by which we can narrow the gap. I have observed that there is some difference between first-generation college graduates (those whose parents did not attend college) and second-generation college graduates (those parents completed college and are generally endowed with and have access to resources).

Second-generation graduates tend to advance more quickly and reach higher levels compared to their first-generation counterparts. There are obvious reasons for this advantage: exposure to their parent's achievements, career mentoring, access to better schools, urban upbringing, family connections, stable housing/mobility, and more. This also suggests that we need another two decades (for first-generation offspring to graduate and become second-generation) before we narrow the gap.

Is there an equalizer?

How can we provide first-generations with access to the same resources and improve their chances? Can we make the playing field more level? What are these resources?

My hypothesis is that mentoring first-generation students can be one of the most effective solutions. Since their parents may not be in a position to provide them with career guidance, they should be able to find it elsewhere. First, there are enlightened Filipinos who have the capacity to mentor bright young kids but are probably unaware that they can help. Second, there are foundations that have funneled their CSR toward academic institutions; these resources could be redirected toward mentoring efforts before graduation. This would be an excellent topic for further research.

What I Love About the Young Generation: An Old Banker's Perspective

I have had the pleasure of working with many young professionals over the last 15 years, as I've mentored many and participated in redesigning management training programs.

Digital Natives and Cultural Transformers: While I am still confused trying to tinker with my laptop and phone apps, they've already figured it out. Their fluency in technology is transformative.

Different, but Dependable: Sure, they have a different way of working. Their workspaces might look like a blend of a tech start-up and a coffee shop. But when they commit to a deadline, they deliver. This is partly because technology allows them to literally work anywhere, often blending their personal and professional lives seamlessly.

Intellectual Hunger: Maybe because there is an abundance of educational materials, they're constantly learning, striving for advanced degrees. I have to add that they define competition differently from my generation, where only one stands as *numero uno*. They collaborate, which is amazing.

Unique Challenges: Apart from the horrendous traffic, the young generation faces problems that were unimaginable in my time, such as commuting in a city overcrowded with cars, finding affordable housing, and managing time so they can take their master's. They adapted by modifying the way they work.

Humble Beginnings, Grand Ambitions: Most of the young professionals I work with come from humble backgrounds. Over 70% of my officers in the bank have parents who didn't attend college. They've overcome significant hurdles to get to where they are today.

The younger generation often gets criticized, but I can't help but admire them. Even now, they are already providing great value because, well, they are different from my generation in a way that adds new perspectives while still keeping the traditional attributes that I hold dear.

The Ideas of March

March is my birth month, and last time, I committed to mentoring 10 young persons on their career development plans. The outcome exceeded my initial expectations. I ended up with 35 mentees, most of whom I have interacted with two to three times. As I returned to school, time management became more challenging, but I found school breaks and holidays useful for continuing this advocacy.

I was not sure if I would be able to make time for them, but what I was sure was that I would do my best to accommodate my commitments. What I contribute as their mentor are stories and lessons I learned from similar situations earlier in my career.

One afternoon, I met three of my mentees, and it was the most diverse afternoon I'd had in a long while. The first gave me an update on his start-up business; he was moving in a direction he preferred and enjoyed. He is a scientist first and foremost but has made a deliberate and commendable effort to learn business skills. The second is a newly graduated computer science major who is starting to make his mark. He is a nerd with an interesting set of diverse skills. We mapped out his next moves. The third is an engineer who decided to specialize in data science. We spent much of the time discussing how he can use his skills to generate value for his employer.

A common theme across the three meetings was the power of intellectual humility—that we need to be ready to learn from our mistakes. We do not assume that we know and that the customer's voice and behavior take precedence. Over coffee and later wine, we did 1-hour sessions each. After that, I always ensure they were introduced to each other, as building a network can help them in the future.

Empty Your Cup

One of my most favorite movie scenes shows an elderly monk pouring tea into an already full cup, deliberately letting it spill on the table. I keep that scene in mind when mentoring or conducting training sessions for young bankers, even if I never mention the movie.

I mentor top-performing youngsters. They topped their classes with Latin honors, had full scholarships, or were student leaders who had already made their mark even before leaving school. Almost all of them have continued to excel at work, in their start-ups, and in graduate school. Half come from the province—a bias I am entitled to, given my background. My mission, and I have chosen to accept it wholeheartedly, is to keep their ascent steady and teach them life's lessons so they remain grounded.

Embracing the concept of an empty cup doesn't mean discarding all previous knowledge and experiences; it just means being open to new information and perspectives and the possibility that what we know to be right may actually be wrong. Sometimes, it means accepting setbacks and mustering the courage to get back on track.

In my mentoring sessions, I emphasize the need to keep learning from three sources, although I adjust the conversation depending on what is more urgent. They must learn from colleagues and the company so they can perform their roles competently and start contributing. Next, they need to pay attention to their customers and never assume they or their organizations already know the customer well enough. And finally, they have to do their homework and prepare for the future by reviewing for the GMAT, for example.

The world is evolving rapidly, and adaptability through lifelong learning is a valuable skill.

Ultimately, an empty cup is bliss. From the time I opened the first Time-Life book on polar exploration, the first Ladybird book on Napoleon, and volume U-V of Grolier's New Book of Knowledge, I was hooked on learning.

"

The stars will never fully align, so raise funding when you can.

Chapter Eleven

Global Curiosity and the Cat

I went to a city that was a significant endpoint for the Silk Road, where everyone spoils the cats. This male cat, Osmanthesecurity, was lounging on the sofa when we arrived, resting from overnight duty, the manager claimed funnily. I am not sure whether he is effective in his work as he is quite friendly. Too friendly, in fact.

At least he was named after an emperor who founded a dynasty that lasted for centuries. That should scare some bad people. After he entered the elevator to show us to our room, my family and I walked 16,000 steps to view the palace grounds, grand mosques, the amazing cistern the Romans built, and the bazaar that sold goods from everywhere.

Sharp Pencils, Sharper Wit

I can't remember exactly when I started the habit of having a cup of sharp pencils as the only permanent fixture on my desk. You may have read previously that I prefer my table neat every start of the day. The pencils were the only exception. Somehow, they reminded me I had to stay sharp.

I usually choose a cup with some sentimental value. I now use one that proudly declares I am an LSE (London School of Economics) Dad, which I shamelessly bought from the school's merchandise store.

The pencils came from all over. Hotels have good ones, although the paint cracks after a couple of years. Island Shang and Marco Polo have some nice blacks. I bought a few from a shop beside the London tube and found a dozen Paul Smiths during a Dubai stopover. And some from Prague.

Growing up, a pencil meant Mongol 2, originally made by Eberhard Faber, whose first factory was in the exact location of the present United Nations Headquarters. It's an interesting piece of trivia. Everyone in Kindergarten had a Mongol and a plastic sharpener. There was joy in seeing the wood peel away as I turned the pencil against the blade. What fascinated me was the large mechanical sharpener that I saw in my father's office. I must have over-sharpened half a dozen pencils just to see how the gears and blades worked.

In high school, we did 4 years of drafting. By that time, we needed various sizes of lead, and other pencil brands became a sign of being a serious draftsman. We went to school with T-squares, triangle rulers, and technical pens.

When I left Citi, my colleagues in Hong Kong gave me an office set that included a stainless steel sharpener. I still have it at home. Recently, as I migrated to an electronic diary and spent entire Saturdays in school, the pencils have taken a backseat.

Recently, I received a nice package from Citi, and I smiled when I saw what was inside. Whoever thought about this, whoever designed this, hit an emotional jackpot.

On the Silk Road

In December 2024, I finally gave in to my curiosity about the Old Silk Road. Too many tales of Marco Polo on Netflix and stories about empires won and lost in the Central Asian states were enough for me to agree to pick Uzbekistan.

From there, I wrote my warm winter greetings from the legendary cities of Samarkand and Bukhara, two historic stops along the Silk Road and centers of great empires. These cities were not only hubs of trade but also birthplaces of groundbreaking advancements in medicine, mathematics, and Islamic theology.

Samarkand, with its stunning architectural brilliance, was a beacon of intellectual exchange. Here, scholars like Al-Khwarizmi developed the foundations of algebra and algorithms, revolutionizing mathematics. The next time I speak about algorithmic leadership, I will be able to trace the origin of the term to a brilliant mathematician from this region and declare that "algorithm" was based on the Latinized version of his name.

Bukhara, with its rich scholarly heritage, was a center for Islamic theology and science during the Golden Age of Islam. *Knowledge enlivens the soul*, said Avicenna (Ibn Sina), a luminary who contributed immensely to medicine and philosophy. Despite being bombed almost beyond recognition by the Red Army in 1920, they have been able to reconstruct their beautiful old city and showcase their craftsmanship.

The region, significantly Persian early on, has seen leadership change hands—sometimes brutally. Despite this, it produced ideas that changed the world. After walking around Bukhara for 3 hours, the only question remaining in my head was why one of every two cars is a white Chevy.

Against the backdrop of a reverse in globalization and the rise of narrow populist interests, I was reminded that the spirit of Samarkand and Bukhara will inspire us all to foster understanding and unity. Let us strive for a world where the exchange of goods and groundbreaking ideas thrives, and where respect for different faiths and races flourishes.

The Power of Taking a Vacation

Do I take vacations? Absolutely! I do, with family, once or twice a year. It's the only time we can all be together. But I seldom use up my allocated days. In fact, aligning everyone's schedules is a logistical challenge. It's like herding cats, but the result is worth it—a blissful escape from the daily grind.

Now, don't get me wrong, I love my job. I enjoy it thoroughly, maybe twice or three times as much as the next guy. But here's a little secret: vacations make me more effective. Let me tell you why.

First, a vacation is like hitting the refresh button on my internal hard drive. It clears away all those pending tasks, stress drops to an all-time low, and my overworked parts get a chance to mend. It's like a necessary reset.

Second, it offers me a chance to step back and think about work in a strategic way. Yes, I might be lounging on a beach, but I'm also absorbing new ideas. I observe how banks operate abroad, watch customer behaviors, and even once saw how Kenyans use mobile phones to settle transactions. These insights are valuable nuggets that I bring back to the office.

Third, life is short. Vacations allow me to make time for the people who matter most. They are the reason I strive to secure a comfortable life. Making memories with loved ones is priceless, and it keeps me motivated.

So yes, I take vacations—but not to "find myself," as social media suggests; not really to see new parts of the world (as I often come back to old favorites); and not to gather new posts for FB (I seldom post about vacations). I travel to be with my sons, who have chosen to build their careers across the globe. Then I come back stronger, smarter, and more inspired.

Extra Virgin Olive Oil and Cheese

I was sitting in a restaurant in Florence when I remembered how I was introduced to Italian cuisine.

When I was a young assistant manager at Citibank, I had a lively crew of four Ateneans working under me. Lunchtimes were our bonding moments, and we often ventured to places they liked. After a Japanese restaurant the day before, we all squeezed into a Mitsubishi Colt and drove to an Italian restaurant. A first for me.

As we settled down, I noticed two mysterious bottles in the middle of the table. One of my colleagues, with the air of a seasoned gourmand, grabbed the bigger bottle and poured some of what looked like oily liquid into a small plate. Then, as if performing a magic trick, he added a few dark drops from the smaller container into the mix. I watched in awe, trying not to look ignorant. The rest of my team followed suit, tearing pieces of bread and dipping them into this concoction.

Curiosity piqued, I observed this ritual with a mix of skepticism. Honestly, I found it a bit peculiar. Nevertheless, I mimicked their actions, not wanting to be the odd one out. To my surprise, the taste was not bad at all. In fact, it was intriguing—a nice blend of simple and sophisticated flavors. I thought, *Ahhh*, this must be what they call *la dolce vita*!

It didn't take long for me to discover that this delightful dip was a mix of olive oil and balsamic vinegar. Add a sprinkle of parmesan, I learned, and the experience was elevated to new heights. This humble combination, which I initially found weird, quickly became a lunchtime favorite.

These lunchtime explorations taught me a lot, not just about food, but about keeping an open mind and embracing new experiences. Who knew that a seemingly ordinary bottle of olive oil could offer such a flavorful lesson in culinary curiosity?

Pineapple on Pizza

As I sat with my colleagues, waiting for our main course to be served, a few waiters started placing small plates of parmesan on the table. I knew it would come in handy for dipping bread in olive oil, a favorite of mine. What intrigued me, though, were the subsequent instructions: *The cheese is not for the seafood.* The waiters repeated this at every table. *The cheese is not for the seafood.* I hadn't ordered seafood, so I wasn't concerned, but my curiosity got the better of me. Later, I Googled it and learned that Italian chefs avoid mixing cheese with seafood because cheese can overpower the delicate seafood flavors. *Ah, that made sense.* I filed away this new piece of culinary thought.

What I still don't get, though, is the debate over pineapples on pizza. I happen to have Hawaiian pizza at the top of my list. Pineapples just have a way of balancing the meaty, cheesy, tomatoey flavors perfectly. However, ordering it in Rome would probably be asking for trouble. As in bodily injury.

As for the cappuccino rule, I had never paid much attention to the "no cappuccino after lunch" guideline. Or is it after 11:00 AM? Either way, it never bothered me, since I stick to my Americano or espresso throughout the day. But in Italy, ordering a cappuccino in the afternoon is a sure way to mark yourself as a tourist. Italians believe that the rich, milky drink is too heavy for post-lunch consumption, preferring a simple espresso.

These dining customs and debates offer a glimpse into the culture and traditions that make each cuisine unique. Some have gone global (some Filipinos have anti-pineapple FB posts). Whether it's respecting the balance of flavors in seafood dishes, enjoying the sweet and savory delight of Hawaiian pizza, or adhering to coffee etiquette, each practice has its own reasons.

Robert De Niro's Waiting

Italy has always fascinated me, even as a child. The allure of Rome, in particular, was captivating. It was the global center of political and military might even before pre-Christian history. Raised on biblical stories, I knew King Herod was appointed by the Romans. The idea that Julius Caesar and his successors walked the very roads we tread today filled me with awe. Rome's streets resonate with the footsteps of history, from emperors to ordinary citizens.

Rome then transitioned to the center of religious influence with the rise of the Roman Catholic Church. Popes and cardinals wielded power that rivaled that of kings. The intricate relationship between church and state shaped the course of European history. Walking through the Vatican and gazing at St. Peter's Basilica, one feels the weight of centuries of religious and political maneuvering. Maybe I just watched too many movies.

Centuries later, Florence, under the stewardship of the Medicis, captured the world's imagination with the Renaissance. This city became a beacon of artistic dominance, home to some of the world's most renowned and unequaled artists. The contributions of Leonardo da Vinci, Michelangelo, and Botticelli continue to inspire and influence art and culture globally. Strolling through the streets, I wonder what Machiavelli was up to when he wrote *The Prince*.

Over the centuries, from military to political, religious, and artistic dominance, Italy has ruled the world in more ways than one. The Renaissance was fueled by a new source of power—financial acumen. The Medicis pioneered banking innovations, including the revolutionary double-entry accounting system. The Florentine Bank of the Medicis employed accountants for their money lending business. You could say that the artistic revival in the Middle Ages had accounting as its secret source of power. Accounting was even compared with mathematics, justice, and the symmetry of God's world. Imagine that!

Being in Italy, where history, religion, and art converge, is an unparalleled experience.

Not a Rock Star

True music believers know that the Elvis hit *It's Now or Never* was translated from *O Sole Mio*, an Italian song. During our dinner one evening, performers serenaded us with the Italian version, led by a singer with a salt-and-pepper mustache that curled at the ends. He was later joined by a soprano, and their voices blended perfectly. I was sure it was not the wine, as I had just started sipping their house red. Maybe the concrete, concave ceiling, built with arches, optimized the experience. The music just overwhelmed us.

Despite our best efforts, we couldn't really belt along, especially during the extended high notes (which the English version, like the one by Elvis, had tamed substantially).

However, the spirit of the evening wasn't lost on us. After over 12,000 steps, up and down the Colosseum, we were justifiably yearning for good food. Okay, we were very hungry. What our partners organized was simply amazing, multiplying our gastronomic satisfaction. Once we got to the bus, you could guess what happened next. We sang to our hearts' content. Yes, even Abba. I may have instigated it, I admit.

There's something magical about singing together, especially when leaders are game and everyone joins in—even if not everyone is perfectly in tune. It made for a fantastic ending to a great day exploring the grandeur that was once Rome.

Back to singing. I am not bashful at all when it comes to music. What I lack in talent, I make up for in confidence, encouraged by two glasses of wine.

Music has a unique way of bringing people together. It breaks barriers and unites individuals in a shared experience. The sing-along on the bus showcased the power of music in building stronger relationships.

Leaders who embrace these moments connect with their colleagues on a personal level. So, next time you find yourself in the company of others, let it go.

When You Gotta Go

Traveling can be an enjoyable experience, whether for business or leisure. However, as we get older, certain aspects of travel become more challenging, particularly when it comes to bladder control. Here are some practical tips to make our journeys more comfortable:

Seize Every Opportunity: Whenever you see a restroom, use it. You never know when you'll find the next one. It's always better to be safe than squirming.

Choose the Right Seat: On a plane, opt for an aisle seat, preferably near but not too close to the restroom. This way, you won't have to climb over other passengers, and you can quickly zoom your way to the toilet when the seatbelt sign is off.

Mind Your Hydration: Avoid overhydration and limit your intake of wine and coffee, as they can increase the need for frequent bathroom trips.

Carry Coins: In Europe, some toilets are coin-operated. Keep one-euro coins handy to avoid any inconvenience. I remember when we couldn't find a restroom in a park in Copenhagen.

Preemptive Strikes: Make it a habit to use the restroom before leaving your hotel room or a restaurant. It's a small step that can save a lot of discomfort later.

Strategic Pit Stops: When you can't find a public toilet, visit a bakery or cafe, buy something small, then use their facilities. I've even pretended to check out merchandise just to access the restroom without making a purchase—then made a quick escape.

I wrote these tips after a lunch with a client where we discussed financing. I shared my "toilet rule" as a metaphor: don't wait for the perfect moment to raise funds. The stars will never fully align, so raise funding when you can.

So, whether it's securing a loan, a bond deal, or finding a restroom, remember: seize the moment.

Missed Saigon

When I heard that Pam Kaur had been appointed as the new HSBC CFO, I sent her a congratulatory note. I remember working for her for a month at Citibank London on a foreign exchange audit. While I spent a lot of time at Lewisham on the outskirts, I also frequently showed up at our headquarters on the Strand—the old business district where the London School of Economics (LSE) still stands. She might recall me wearing bowties for weeks.

Every time I got out of work, I exited through the door that faced Drury Lane, the theater where Miss Saigon was then showing. I would stop for a few seconds, smiling with Filipino pride as Lea Salonga was top billing the show. Then, I would remind myself that I was still saving money and start walking to the train station.

That time, I had just gotten married and taken a mortgage for our first home. I would grab a sandwich on the way, which I'd later eat back at the hotel while typing away my notes on my very clunky IBM laptop. It was so heavy that going to the gym wasn't necessary.

Despite my admiration for Lea Salonga, I never watched the show there. The show ran several times in Manila years later, but by then, I was already based in Singapore and other parts of Asia, so I just forgot about it.

It's funny how certain news and places can trigger memories. That door facing Drury Lane was my daily reminder of what I was missing, not just a theatrical masterpiece, but a celebration of Filipino talent on a global stage. When I visited my younger son at LSE years ago, I had the same feeling of euphoria, but also a reminder of the time I needed to balance my budget and commitments.

Hopefully, one day, I'll get another chance to see it—this time, without a heavy laptop or a strict budget holding me back.

"

Time is my most important currency.

Chapter Twelve

Don't be Boring

As a banker, I had to follow prescribed dress codes. To be honest, having uniforms made it easy to prepare in the morning—I didn't have to waste my time thinking of what combination to put on. However, soon after I joined Citibank, I noticed that not everyone complied; there was always some senior person who exhibited his own style.

When I was senior enough, I started experimenting. At some point, I wore bow ties for a whole week. And then argyles and other colored socks followed. While I deviated from dressing norms because they were too boring, I was still, for the most part, obedient.

When I Dyed My Hair Blonde

When I was Treasurer of Citi Philippines, there was a time when the markets were getting boring, but the budget needed to be met. One day, while sitting in my corner of the trading desk, I uttered the fatal words, "If we make X million dollars, I will dye my hair blonde."

Across the trading desk, Paul Favila jumped and screamed, "DONE!"

Paul was my Trading Head, close comrade, and lunchmate. We worked together in Singapore before coming back for senior assignments in Manila. (He is now the country CEO.)

Naturally, Paul and the desk heads made it happen. And I had to deliver on my promise.

One day, while on leave, I quietly went to Franck Provost salon in Alabang and explained what needed to be done. I then put on my Switzerland cap and went to the bank.

When I got off the lift, the first person I saw was an American expat who did not know how to react seeing me with hair blonder than his.

The trading room at the tenth became a crazy place over the next couple of hours. Word went around the building, and people came from all over, bringing cameras. Cameras! This was before phones had them. I must have posed for at least 50 takes.

Then we had lunch. At that time, I was a newly minted Managing Director with two unopened bottles of Dom Perignon. It seemed the right time to pop them.

After the sanity set in, I left for the salon, and they knew exactly what for, but not before we had another half dozen pics to mark the occasion.

After that, no one doubted my word. My word was my blonde, I mean, my bond.

Wear Red Pants

Wearing green is easy, as it pairs quite well with many colors. But red? Red for men takes courage. We can wear red shirts easily, but red pants require a whole lot more, well, introspection. A bit of rebellion, perhaps?

You have to start by asking yourself why you are even considering this bold fashion choice. Does it diminish you in any way? Is it worth the trouble? Can you carry it? The answers might vary, but when it is Christmas, the situation changes. It might be worth it, especially if the invitation says to wear something red.

Actually, the question should start with why did you even buy the red pants in the first place? What were you thinking? My answer: they were on sale, and I might plead temporary insanity. I bought them, so I might as well find an occasion to wear them.

Matching red pants can be tricky. Don't pair them with green unless you want to look like a walking holly wreath or Christmas tree. Instead, go with neutral colors to keep the outfit cool. Plain black or dark blue shirts or even a classic white shirt work well with red pants. Then choose a cream or navy blazer. As for footwear, brown loafers or plain shoes are great choices that complement and balance the overall look. The key is to let the red pants have their day, and all other articles of clothing play a supporting role.

To illustrate, I once attended a grand celebration somewhere in North Luzon. I decided to wear bright red pants, an oxford button-down white shirt, and brown loafers. The outfit allowed me to blend into a sea of people wearing the same color, one with them in embodying the holiday spirit. My bright red pants were proof that I was not a boring banker and brought a sense of Christmas cheer wherever I went.

Son of a Beach

I was born in Cebu but grew up in Eastern Mindanao. Our barrio, Mangagoy, faced the Pacific on one side, with a lush forest behind us. I could literally walk to the shore from school; the forest was right next door.

Sadly, the barrio's coastline wasn't clean enough for swimming. The public market was right next to it, along with the pier, or *pantalan*, which was deep enough for shallow fishing boats. We had to go a bit farther to find a nicer, cleaner place for picnics or drive for half an hour to get to Barcelona Beach, where the water was calmer, and we could practice our strokes.

Otherwise, the waves on our side weren't exactly gentle with young children. They were taller than us, so we would run up and down the sand as if the waves were chasing us. We had never heard of surfing before. If we had, I might be a surfer dude by now. Maybe that's why I was never a beach guy. I'm okay hanging out with a good book, but I'm not crazy about the sand and the sea. Maybe I just take them for granted.

What the sea does, though, is clear my mind. I remember staring at the horizon, composing new strategies and memos in my head. Beaches are my thinking spots. This is not original. I remember John Reed of Citibank, who wrote the famous *Memo from the Beach*, outlining the bank's consumer banking focus and ATM network. Interestingly, he insisted on two machines per branch in case one would fail. I've written at least four such memos in the four banks I've been associated with.

I once spoke to the Asia management team of our insurance partner, whose leaders are sunny and full of life. Reflecting on my journey as I stared from the balcony, I realized that while I may not be a beach enthusiast, the sea has always been a source of clarity.

Life Is an Ultra Marathon

Being competitive and sprinting through life has its pluses and a lot of minuses. While it brings moments of glory, it also comes with low points. What it surely does is wear you down early.

Grad school in the 80s was like a series of sprints. Citibank's Executive Trainee program (later renamed Management Associate) was designed for young talent on the fast track to promotion—rising from assistant manager to vice president in just 7 years (now even faster, after I worked with HR in 2005 to start hiring at the manager level). You either met the standard or you didn't. Thankfully, the vast majority did.

Treasury was another hyper-competitive place where information absorption was tremendous. And the tribe had first-class talent. You had to keep up with the pace.

How do you survive and thrive in such an environment? By getting 8 hours of sleep daily, putting in extra work on weekends to reduce workload during the week, being with supportive colleagues, and having an understanding family.

I seldom compromise on my sleep hours. When I had to, my body collected extra hours of sleep during weekends and charged interest. Even during my MBA, I stayed in the dorm and slept at 11:00 PM; I woke up at 7:00 AM.

I don't play golf, so I can read in peace during the weekend or have some extra thinking time. And I admit I really read ahead of schedule. My DBA professor once laughed when he recalled I sent him a note about a topic we would cover in 2 weeks. He did not know I had already enjoyed reading the whole semester's material.

The most important thing is, you can't compete alone. You get farther with family and friends. Family makes it worthwhile and adds spring to your step. In school on Saturdays, my classmates and I help each other out. When I miss something, someone is ready to help out. Quickly.

APT, APT.

I have been singing the refrain of this song (where you repeat "apateu" six times) ever since I watched Rosé and Bruno Mars perform this on YouTube. Why do songs have such stickiness? Apparently, our favorite songs blast into multiple parts of our brain, making it latch on almost permanently. If it is emotional, it makes you want to move, and if it has a rhythmic beat, it is hard to forget.

With a tight schedule and my book launch one weekend, the lines from the APT song (Rosé & Mars, 2024) hit the spot. The new hit picks some of the 80's song's refrain beat, which is why the latter's composers were credited as co-composers of APT. (I Googled this!)

In grade four science class, we were taught about vitamins and their best food sources. Well, I was never a fan of enumeration, and as early on, I found it a waste of thinking time. I remedied this annoyance by entertaining myself. One way was to turn this seemingly random information into something easily retrievable. What are the best sources of Vitamin B? According to the teacher, and I now list them in the exact same sequence: cabbages, potatoes, beans, tomatoes, squash leaves, cashews, chicos, mangoes, unpolished rice, eggs, and milk.

How did I manage to remember this sequence until now, half a century later? I sang it to the tune of *Auld Lang Syne* (Burns, 1788). Try singing it, and you will never forget. By the way, the Scot song teaches us to cherish old memories, so it does make sense to use it to remember a lesson in grade four.

When Kids Stop Believing in Santa

According to studies, kids start questioning their parents at 8 years old. Around this time, kids begin to be skeptical about Santa in school; they become more aware of the magnitude of the world's population of children, and the sheer volume of work that needs to be accomplished.

And yes, adults screw up, like the time my son noticed that I used wrapping paper from Borders on a medium-sized teddy bear. Upon his instructions, I even wrote an email to santaclaus@northpole.com and gave my son the printed reply that ended with "ho ho ho."

On Christmas Eve, we left out a glass of milk and a plate of cookies. Before midnight, for good measure, I sneaked over to take a sip of the milk and bit into one of the cookies. Check. I thought the partially eaten cookie strategy was a stroke of genius. Since we had no chimney in our Singapore flat, I was ready with the perfect story—Santa entered through the balcony. Check!

But the wrapping paper gave it away, and my son, who was seven then, started to have doubts even though he liked his Christmas teddy bear.

A 2024 study by Mills et al. (2024), *Debunking the Santa Myth: The Process and Aftermath of Becoming Skeptical About Santa*, published in *Developmental Psychology*, surveyed 383 adult participants. On average age, they reported discovering the truth at the age of 8.5 (ranging from 3 to 13, which was quite wide). The majority (67%) learned about it by overhearing a classmate talk about Santa.

How did they react? Well, 51.7% felt sadness, 13.1% felt pride, and 10.2% felt anger. Negative emotions did not last long, and respondents did not recall a lack of trust in their parents.

Finally, the study asked a further question: If participants had children, would they teach their children about Santa? A high 90.1% said they would.

And that is why the tradition goes on.

A Sucker Posts Every Minute

One of my pet peeves is supposedly well-educated individuals with respectable jobs posting or sharing false news or advice. Some of those I've corrected say they do it out of their concern for their friend's safety. They claim to be acting out of the goodness of their hearts.

These ridiculous stories can be easily debunked with a quick search. But they argue, "What if it is true? What if Facebook was going to start charging?

Then, there are those who dig deeper to find more information from fellow believers supporting their position. Naturally, their echo chambers provide them with more "evidence," so they can keep convincing each other.

What is the root cause of these behaviors? Perhaps belief without critical thinking. Generations have been shaped by an educational system that emphasizes memorization and obedience over intellectual discourse. The scientific method, which I learned in first year high school, insists that any statements purported to be true should be tested, and we should attempt to disprove them.

So, what is the root cause? Intellectual pride, maybe. A refusal to listen to new facts, accept new reasoning, or consider new sources of information.

The prevalence of these sucker posts is a modern-day hyperabundance of misinformation. The irony of "doing it out of the goodness of their hearts" is that it often does more harm than good. False news spreads panic, misinformation can lead to dangerous behavior, and baseless advice can have dire consequences.

The solution? A return to critical thinking. Question everything, especially if it aligns perfectly with your pre-existing beliefs. It's about being responsible.

In the end, it's about fostering a culture of truth and reason. And maybe, just maybe, if we all start thinking a little more critically, we can turn the tide against these sucker posts once and for all.

So, next time you see a dubious post, channel your inner Sherlock Holmes and do some sleuthing. Remember, sharing is caring—but only if what you're sharing won't make your friends roll their eyes. Let's make the Internet a smarter place, one post at a time!

Clean Desk or Messy Desk

I used to work for someone I greatly admired for his intellect and wisdom. Every now and then, I would need to discuss a deal with him. I would sit across from him with his fire hazard of a desk between us. Half the time, I would ask him why his table was inches deep with folders and piles of paper. His answer was always that he knew where everything was. It was messy but, if you looked hard enough, it was organized. There was some pattern in the organized chaos. Okay, I said. Then, I would pester him again the next month. This certifiable genius preferred a messy desk. This, in fact, has been stereotyped.

To help settle this issue in my head, I looked for material that would give me some clarity. I found a study by psychology scientist Kathleen Vohs and her fellow researchers (Vohs, Redden and Rahinel, 2013) at the University of Minnesota, published in *Psychological Science*, a journal of the Association for Psychological Science. In brief, the ones who were more orderly were more likely to engage in socially responsible behavior. The ones from a messy room generated ideas that were judged as more creative by an independent panel. In other words, it is not binary "all or nothing;" it was being "more of."

That made me feel better. You see, I generally keep an orderly desk, well-arranged files, and a sharply organized schedule. All three allow me to be more productive and effective, and see much action in a week. More importantly, I do not miss important things. At least, at the start and end of the day, my desk looks neat. But during the day is another story, as there tends to be a bit of chaos with folders and papers, with cups of coffee, and a plate of chicken wings (garlic parmesan from Yellow Cab) on the side. I eat lunch at my desk if I have no meetings. Again, by the time I leave, the desk is neat.

What really matters is that you do what works for you. Anyway, keep a fire extinguisher on standby.

No Sleep? Start Counting

There are only a few good reasons I don't get sufficient sleep, like doing a Netflix marathon or chasing a deal over a short period. Even then, I make sure to catch up with naps whenever I can. Otherwise, I will not be able to fully dedicate myself at work.

In my case, I need 8 hours of sleep daily. But when Song Hye-kyo came out in *The Glory*, that dropped to six. I made up for it by dozing off during the weekend. *The Glory Part Two* will probably result in the same lack of sleep.

If you live a hectic life, you will need to step back and reorganize. Do the math. Start counting. Ask yourself which activities are consuming much of your time and do three things:

1. Delegate or outsource: If you can, have your laundry done outside, order packed meals, Grab instead of drive, or pay a part-time cleaner. I did some of these when I was based abroad.

2. Eliminate or reschedule low-priority activities: Try to cut out the low-priority activities or move some of your time-insensitive activities to the weekend.

3. Restructure to save time: Live closer to the office if possible. Work from home. Cut your hair short. Simplify your wardrobe. Watch digital YouTubes while walking on the treadmill. Go to a gym next door before going to work; don't go far so you don't have to bring too much stuff.

Not having to drive adds one and a half hours of productive time. Having a meeting over lunch saves at least half an hour. Simplifying wardrobe routine (like no French cuffs and avoiding ties at times) saves maybe 15 minutes.

When I was taking my MBA, I studied ahead during weekends. That way, I slept well during the class week and was fresh for battles in the classroom.

Juggling Time

Time management is an issue for those who have many activities they want to accomplish. It sometimes becomes an issue for me, although somehow, I have found a system. Maybe I am used to this because I was like this in high school and college—except that, instead of work, I had studies, extracurriculars, and other interests. How do I make it work?

Apart from the ultra-busy job of running a bank and its subsidiaries, I am actively involved in three school boards. On the side, I am an author and a DBA student at AIM. How do I manage to juggle everything?

Firstly, outside of family, work is my top priority. When there is conflict, work comes first, and my studies come second. It helps that I have vacation leave credits, which I can mark ahead for mandatory school attendance.

Secondly, I take advantage of technology. When I need to be absent from class, I catch up by watching the recorded lectures. Since I often read the cases ahead of time, I can send my insights to the professor.

Thirdly, I have decided to avoid certain time-consuming activities, like golf or cycling. I tried them before, but while they suit my friends, I couldn't sustain my interest. I say no to invitations so I can focus on what I need to do.

Fourth, and most importantly, I plan ahead. If I have a keynote speech, the draft script and slides are completed weeks in advance. I also schedule my homework and paper submission in my calendar. I complete them ahead of time, usually during Sundays (I have classes most Saturdays). I don't have to submit them beforehand, but I have time to think about them and make further edits if necessary. No stress from cramming.

Time is my most important currency. I spend it as well as I can. I save enough so I can have that annual vacation with my family, now that my boys are halfway across the globe.

Hairodynamic: The Advantages of Having Less Hair

My genius friend Cris (he has a PhD and two master's degrees from MIT) was once teased by our follically gifted classmates about why he paid the standard charge at the barber when, like me, he had less hair. His answer was a stroke of, well, genius. He replied, "Degree of difficulty!"

Thinning hair became an issue for me when my math classmates first noticed that the top of my head was showing more skin. I was sixteen then. A similarly challenged dorm roommate and I decided to take matters into our own hands. We harvested some gelatinous herbs from the university garden (they were in abundance) and applied them every evening before taking a shower. It was messy.

Now that I am old and gray, it is less of an issue. The best solution? It is now best addressed by cutting hair short for a *hairodynamic*, sleek, and youngish look. The downside is that I need to wear a hat when going to western countries during winter or fall; otherwise, I will catch a cold.

The upside is I consume much less shampoo, barely need to dry my hair, and have no use for a comb. I save time. That should add up to hours and days saved, which I can redirect to more productive activities. I feel bad for those who have thick hair; they must feel miserable. Or not.

I am not about to grow a lot of hair on one side and wallop it over on top. I see some guys doing that, but that isn't my thing. That would be too obvious and would mark me as a banker for doing a "savings-and-loan" strategy.

My strategy now calls for a quick 3-2-1 cut when visiting the barber. That's what I say exactly: 3 for the top, 2 on the side, and 1 near the ear. That is the classification of the electric shears that they all use.

ASK THE CEO

Part Four

Solving Society's Challenges

"

Complaining does not move the needle. What works is when individuals do what they can, in their current roles, and make the change.

Chapter Thirteen

Inequality and Inclusion

Sadly, there are enough stories in Philippine history and in today's society to illustrate inequality—from the friars and Spaniards who owned vast tracts of land then and those they regarded as poor Indios who worked the fields—to news of continuing inequalities fueled by factors such as limited access to education and healthcare for marginalized groups.

Power. Land. Even more power. Revolutions and wars have been fought over them. Movies have created many stars using the same formula. And some of those stars even became presidents and senators.

We should not wait for some bigger authority to solve society's problems. Complaining does not move the needle. What works is when individuals take action within their current roles and make the change.

What Are You, Other Than a Banker?

A new friend, aware I had just turned 60, posed that question the other day. I cannot remember exactly how he ended up asking me, but it might have been because of my post entitled *Don't Die Twice*.

He is nearly as old as I am. We were shooting the breeze around lunchtime after my speech, munching on small cakes. I stared at him for a few seconds. I answered, *Maybe an educator*. I explained that I served on the boards of my high school, university and graduate school and was keenly involved in financial sustainability, academic innovation, and giving opportunities to the less fortunate.

It just jumped out of my thoughts. Maybe what I am is what I do and why I do it. I could have said "mentor" or "author," but I did not. Perhaps because both fall under the general umbrella of education, fulfilling the same objective.

The next day, I sat beside a university president, a gentleman I greatly admire. Our discussion started with naval architecture and engineering (he is the foremost expert on the subject in the country) and how it relates to faster swimming. Later on, we switched to credits per student and other quantitative measures that indicate the business efficiency of universities. It turned into a half-hour discussion on optimization of academic resources. I was hooked on both topics.

Then there is this related issue of being "global." I am not. I am writing this because I see the word "global" frequently enough, and it got me thinking. At best, I am regional, as I used to cover Asia derivatives structuring for Citi from India to Taiwan. Also, I was chair of Asian Bankers Association for 2 years. Maybe I can call myself "international," but never the G-word. And I actually worked in Global Markets as a managing director, but only led one cluster. I spent weeks working in London and the United States in my earlier years, but it wasn't long enough and not permanent.

Glocal?

Equalizing Through Education

When I was an infant, my father moved our family in Eastern Mindanao to join a new company. He later told me that one of the biggest reasons was the private school set up to provide city-level education for the company's dependents.

Apart from having teachers recruited by the Maryknoll nuns, we also received excellent technical education—sheet metal projects, electrical tasks, woodworking, and 4 years of drafting. Then, the La Salle Brothers supervised the school midway. They hired honor graduates from a Jesuit school.

My classmates and I performed creditably during our university studies, mainly due to the excellent elementary and secondary preparations we had. We were lucky. Social strata hardly mattered back home. Many of my classmates obtained scholarships.

Not everyone gets this chance, even though the La Salle Brothers have made it their mission to improve the quality of schools through formal supervision. I believe they oversee more than a hundred private schools. This is why I have found serving on the boards of two La Salle schools a worthwhile advocacy.

Continuing this story, I later found myself in another position to pay forward. During my first CEO assignment, we implemented a management training program that selected leaders and honor graduates from various schools across the country and put them through a four-month bootcamp—the Junior Executive Development Institute or JEDI. Over a hundred graduated from the program, many of whom now work with me. My hope was that the intensive course would add skills and confidence to those from provincial schools or humble backgrounds, helping them compete better against the top Manila universities.

Fast forward to our Bank, where our HR continues this practice. We even started a part-time management development program for those already in permanent positions. The program is called TOPGUN.

A Recipe for Resentment

Inequity builds resentment and can become potentially explosive, especially if the following conditions exist: the privileged class mistreats the lower classes or grants unfair advantages to their own; the privileged class hasn't done anything to deserve their level of comfort—they were either born into it or never worked for it; and there is no perceived opportunity for the lower class to improve their situation, leaving them forever stuck where they are.

So, what do we do? I have few suggestions:

1. Make school entry based on aptitude, without giving priority to children or siblings of alumni. Education should be a meritocracy, where the best and brightest have access to the best opportunities, regardless of familial connections.

2. Accelerate the improvement of academic standards in state universities and colleges. By raising the quality of education in public institutions, we provide more students with the tools they need to succeed. This benefits not only the students but also society as a whole.

3. Distribute the centers of excellence across three times as many regions, similar to how we have over 70 science high schools nationwide. We also have to ensure that educational opportunities are not concentrated in a few urban areas. This ensures that talented students from all over the country have access to quality education.

4. Provide state subsidies for teachers' salaries in top-performing private schools that keep their fees affordable. This would incentivize private schools to maintain high academic standards without passing the costs on to students.

By ensuring that educational opportunities are based on merit, improving public education, distributing resources equitably, and supporting educators, we can create a more just and equitable society.

First-Generation College Graduates

By first-generation, I refer to students whose parents do not have college degrees. I first came across this issue when I reviewed the family backgrounds of the officers we hired. Over time, I began to see a pattern and asked Human Resources to compile the data.

I found out that only half of the sampled applicants declared their parent's occupations. Based on those who did, and given the substantial sample size, we were able to infer that over 70% were first-generation graduates.

We all know that the academic experience of first-generation college students can be significantly different compared to that of their second-generation counterparts. I could not find local research, but I came across a study of Cataldi, Bennett and Chen (2018), published by the National Center for Education Statistics. According to their research, first-generation students are more likely to attend less prestigious institutions. Post-graduation, these individuals are limited by a lack of professional networks and mentorship opportunities.

In contrast, as a second-generation, I benefited from my parents' resources and guidance, not just from them but also from their network of friends. Still, coming from the province, my resources paled in comparison to those of my classmates in graduate school who were raised in urban Metro Manila.

I scanned through more western research. A Pew Research Center (2021) analysis of the *2019 Survey of Household Economics and Decision-Making* showed a 60.8% gap in household wealth between the first-generation and second-generation graduates.

To bridge this gap, interventions are essential. Personally, the first crucial intervention in my life was AIM's career development services, which opened my eyes to vast possibilities.

Research recommends similar solutions to provide knowledge resources and guidance to first-generation students as early as their college years. By understanding these disparities and implementing targeted interventions, we can help first-gens reach their full potential, fostering a more inclusive and equitable society.

First Generation Students; Harvard Lessons

One weekend, I had the privilege of having coffee with Harvard professor Jill Avery to discuss an exciting financial inclusion project for HBS MBA students. After covering the main topic, I mentioned our new advocacy for first-generation college graduates and expressed how passionate we are about it.

I explained that over three-quarters of our new junior officers come from first-generation backgrounds. Many have fathers who are drivers, farmers, and manual workers, while their mothers are primarily housewives, with a few managing a small store or wet market stall.

We are committed to mentoring, starting with the top-performing ones, to ensure they have access to valuable advice, guidance, and all the advantages their parents may not be able to provide, but a mentor can. This support system is important for their development and success, and should ideally be available even to unproven new hires.

Jill listened intently with a wide smile. It turns out she was a first-generation college graduate herself. (When I Googled, I found that 20% of Harvard students are first-generation.) Jill is deeply involved in supporting these students and hosts AMA (Ask Me Anything) sessions, where first-generations, in a safe setting, can quickly move up the learning curve. I found this approach brilliant and thought it would be a great practice for us to adopt.

Emboldened by our conversation, I sent out a memo shortly after about a new initiative tentatively called *Project 1GEN*. The program aims to inspire and support first-generation officers by encouraging personal and professional growth, empowering them with mentorship, and helping them build strong networks. We believe this initiative will make a significant difference on their careers and contribute to their long-term success.

The goal is to create an inclusive environment where first-generation graduates can reach their full potential.

Digital Financial Inclusion

We chose our advocacies carefully. Inspired by the values of our bank founder (Ambassador Alfonso Yuchengco), nation-building has always been part of our DNA. We decided to put some activism in banking; financial inclusion through digital banking was our first advocacy.

We knew that financial inclusion was one way of helping Filipinos escape the poverty trap. Unfortunately, the traditional manual methods were too costly and not scalable. The more efficient way was through digital apps. So, we decided to launch not just one, or two, but three platforms and apps focused on the countryside and small businesses.

Apart from our main mobile app, we have DiskarTech, which is in Taglish and purpose-built for the underserved market. There's also ATMGo, a handheld POS machine that allows over 7,000 grocery owners and coop offices across the country to offer ATM withdrawals and other basic formal banking services. We have reached almost every single town in the country, and our main users are government employees. Finally, there is BOZ, which is designed for small business owners. It can process payments, do simple payroll, send invoices, and track collections, freeing up time for entrepreneurs. We had to change the spelling because we were told that a retailer complained.

We did not forget the workers who often end up borrowing from their friendly neighborhood five-sixers (borrow five, pay six in a week). Through our mobile app Pulz, customers with payroll accounts with us can, within two minutes, advance a portion of their salary and repay in two installments. No need to leave the office to go to the branch.

In our first year, we also started winning the award for Best Bank in Digital Banking. We've held on to it for the last 5 years.

"

Each individual
needs to
moderate their
buying behavior.
If we keep buying,
someone will
keep producing.
Buy, but buy
moderately.

Chapter Fourteen

Serious with Sustainability

In 2020, we declared that we would withdraw our support for new coal power plants and focus our funding on renewable energy projects. It was personal as well. I was trained as a physicist in college and had been a renewable energy junkie since grade six. It felt like I was coming back to something I really found fulfilling.

It took 2 years before another bank followed our declaration; they were dead serious about it as we were.

And then, as I arrived at the office 1 day, a thoughtful colleague left a small box containing a Nespresso technical pencil, made from one capsule of recycled aluminum, with the lead partly produced from recycled coffee grounds. Simply awesome.

The Buying Man

There are so many things we seem to need nowadays. And it is so easy to find them.

Before, the rubber shoes I used for school were the same ones for every sport. Now, there is a specific shoe for each activity. If you play tennis, badminton, golf, running and go to the gym, that adds up to five pairs. Even for running, there are at least three different shoe structures depending on how your feet move. The correct shoe prevents injury, provides bounce or traction when appropriate, and optimizes performance, as stated in the shoe box.

Fast Fashion. Fashion used to be a yearly thing. In Western countries, it was seasonal. During a case study 10 years ago, I was amazed when my professor showed how global value chains could run new designs within a month. The only thing that hasn't changed is the short-sleeve, light blue, button-down oxford shirt. Actually, no—it is now available in dozen other colors. You can actually request it in dark blue, white, khaki, maroon, mint green, and so on. You get my point.

Planned Obsolescence. Every 3 years, we need to update our phones and laptops. If we don't, they won't be able to handle new apps or have enough capacity to run efficiently. You can stretch it a bit longer, but eventually, you'll have to donate or ditch them.

Fast fashion and planned obsolescence are real, successful business strategies that make Homo Emptor buy unlimited goods. Now, you don't even have to go to the shops. You just order from your phone. No traffic, no need to leave the house. The downside? Unnecessary depletion of resources, accelerated waste accumulation, and single-use plastic packaging. All these purchases, unless reused, eventually end up in landfills.

Each individual needs to moderate their buying behavior. If we keep buying, someone will keep producing. Buy, but buy moderately.

Don't Buy the Jacket

When I turned 60, I told myself that I had enough clothes and shoes to last the rest of my life. After all, I take great care of my possessions. All I need to do is keep my waistline in check.

One weekend, I happened to pass by a store near where I live. Displayed right next to the entrance was a canvas jacket in olive green with dark brown collar. I stood about two meters in front of it and stared for what must have been at least three minutes. I examined every single detail without touching it. I couldn't explain why this particular piece of garment captured my attention.

It was only later when I remembered that, over three decades ago, I found a similar jacket in the bargain section of a department store and got it for a fifth of its original price.

I could have told you it was my go-to jacket, but I can't, because for at least a decade, it was my only one. It was not like I had another option. Over time, it wore down until the collar was wrinkled beyond repair. It took me a while before I decided to give it away. I should have remembered that while I was in the shop, but I did not. So, I resolved to finally go and get it next day after work.

Fast forward to the following evening, I was about to change into casual clothes, preparing to fetch the prize. As I was taking off my white shirt, I stopped, realizing the error of my ways. I was about to give in to the folly of fashion, relishing some sentimental story that was best buried in the past.

I grabbed the brown blazer hanging outside the corner of the closet. I told myself that I had what I needed, and wore it instead 2 days later. I did not need another jacket to relive the past.

Bark to the Past

Every time I pass by the hundreds of eucalyptus trees planted beside the expressway, two memories come to mind.

First, that planting fast-growing eucalyptus trees right next to highways is a terrible idea. These trees, classified as softwood, are notorious for breaking easily during typhoons. This explains why you often see them cut halfway, a constant reminder of their vulnerability and the potential hazard they pose during storms. Despite this, they are undeniably beautiful, with their trunks displaying a spectrum of colors.

Second, I grew up right next to a paper mill and lumber yard. The raw material used consisted of softwood trees grown in thousands of hectares of tree farms. Among these were bagras (eucalyptus deglupta) and falcata (albizia falcataria), primarily used for newsprint, and Caribbean pines (Pinus caribaea), which were used for a higher-quality white paper. This was the information imparted to us during educational tours, although that was 50 years ago.

You might think my childhood was steeped in the scent of fresh timber and the rhythmic hum of the mill's machinery. Actually, not quite. For some reason, there was a particular smell that often emanated from the plant site, and it was not exactly pleasant. We used to say that the company owner had passed gas! (God bless his soul.)

Traveling to other towns, we would pass by rows upon rows of well-organized green. The reforestation efforts were so systematic and efficient. My classmates and I did a yearly bus ride and trek to areas deep in the forest concession to do tree planting. These experiences instilled in me a deep appreciation for the balance between industry and nature.

It's fascinating how certain landscapes can evoke such vivid memories and reflections. Every eucalyptus tree I pass by reminds me of a time when life was simpler, the air was fresher, and every journey held a lesson in sustainability.

My Green Wish

One weekend, I walked over to a nearby Fully Booked bookstore. When the lady was about to put my purchase into a plastic bag, I cringed and stopped her. I told her I'd just show the receipt to the guard on my way out. Not long before that, during a customer event we organized, I gave a non-negotiable order: *No plastic bottles of water.*

I have only one person to "blame," Professor Felipe Calderon, who had us reading over 200 pages of well-curated articles on sustainability. I have realized that, despite our radical approaches—like being the first bank to publicly declare withdrawal of support for coal plants in 2020 and building rich pipeline of renewable energy projects—we were merely scratching the surface.

Here are my thoughts:

First, a declaration of intent, like setting a target for becoming carbon neutral, should be encouraged, even if the company is just starting its journey. I believe that declaration is the equivalent of making a U-turn, or at least the public signaling of one. I will, through public events and LinkedIn posts, encourage them to take the plunge and prepare their plans. Even small efforts, like switching the building's power to renewable energy or launching an educational campaign to raise employees' awareness of their carbon footprint, should be celebrated.

In our company, we are midway in quantifying the greenhouse gas emissions across our portfolio. Using our pipeline of renewable energy projects and other considerations, we are hoping to mathematically estimate when we will achieve carbon neutrality.

Additionally, we organize industry events where sustainability practices are shared. We've been doing this annually. Recently, we invited Professor Mahar Lagmay, who leads Project NOAH (Nationwide Operational Assessment of Hazards), as speaker. He clearly and concisely described climate change to media participants, connecting it to our work and everyday lives to make the discussion more meaningful. He also showed that Metro Manila's elevation has been sinking because of ground water extraction.

Digital banking is my chosen research topic. I have been convinced to add a chapter on sustainability in my dissertation. Digitization, in itself, has shifted over-the-counter (OTC) transactions to our mobile app. This has reduced the need for physical facilities and lowered utility expenses. We have been able to close 40 of our branches over the last 3 years, saving on expenses as almost 90% of our transactions are now done digitally or through ATMs and cards. This has also reduced the need for our customers to drive to our branches.

Most of us hope for a greener world. While this is not an easy task and there are competing issues that need to be balanced, it has to be one of our highest priorities. What is important is that we start moving in the right direction as early as possible.

Don't Drink Water

Not from a plastic bottle.

— It takes 450 years for plastic bottles to decompose, and 20 years for plastic bags.

— Single-use plastics account for 50% of plastic waste in landfills (NOAA, 2021).

— Only 9% of plastic gets recycled; 80% end up in landfills, and the rest are burned.

— Up to 80% of marine debris is plastic, almost entirely coming from land sources.

— Plastic degrades into microplastics and enters the food chain through seafood and salt (Kibria et al., 2023).

Plastic technology was developed in the 1940s. They remain popular as they are light, cheap and durable. They are mostly derived from petroleum, although there are new types made from agriculture products.

The huge volume of plastic waste is already an ongoing ecological disaster. They poison the soil, contaminate ground water, and clog our drainage systems. I even read about a study claiming microplastics have been found in the human brain.

I recently listened to two presentations on how plastic waste can be converted into an alternative energy source, and I was impressed. After all, new technologies can break down plastics. I also read a journal article on plastics by Kibria, et al. (2023) which was a supplementary reading material for our class. I learned that our inability to efficiently recycle means we need to focus on controlling them at the source, not at the tail end.

Firstly, we have to reduce our consumption of plastic products, especially single-use plastics. Drink water from a glass or a flask instead. Reuse as much as possible (though keep in mind that some plastics start degrading when reused). Then, set them aside for recycling.

In the play *Julius Caesar* by Shakespeare (1599), there is this line: *The evil that men do lives after them; the good is oft interred with their bones*. I can liken this to plastic bottles and how they linger, for 450 years, yes, this long. *The plastic bottle that men drink from lives after them; the waste is oft interred in landfills*.

Top Ocean Plastic Polluter

Republic Act No. 11898, or Extended Producer Responsibility (EPR) Act of 2022, is the operative Philippine law for controlling plastic pollution and stopping the country from being the leading ocean plastic polluter in the world.

The EPR Act aims to achieve plastic neutrality, which, as defined in the legislation, is *a system or its desired outcome where, for every amount of plastic product footprint created, an equivalent amount thereof is recovered or removed from the environment by the product producers through an efficient waste management system.*

It requires large companies to take responsibility for the entire lifecycle of their plastic products, especially after consumption. The target starts with 20% recovery, increasing to 80% over the next 4 years.

I checked how companies, especially the top plastic polluters, were doing. A European firm impressively achieved plastic neutrality almost immediately with its deliberate plastic collection programs, surpassing its FMCG peers. However, a quick scan shows that they burn the plastic in kilns, although in a controlled environment, as part of the cement manufacturing process. Another company, which shall not be named, seems to be taking its sweet time.

The real challenge, I think, lies in single-use sachets and plastic bottles. Since the latter remains the most economical method of packaging, billions are produced yearly. At only 100 bottles per person per year, the total adds up to 11 billion—and there's probably much more. Since studies show low collection and recycling rates, we need to pay more attention on how we can control plastic usage at the source, at the purchase decision stage. Why are we buying more plastic-packaged products?

And if that means giving up on some of life's refreshing pleasures, so be it.

Drink Coffee Responsibly

If you're a coffee lover, consider this: every time you grab that morning espresso in a disposable cup, you are likely adding to the growing plastic pollution crisis. While that paper cup convenience is tempting, the environmental cost is steep.

Disposable coffee cups may seem harmless, but they are often lined with plastic to prevent leakage. This type of plastic is notorious for its longevity, taking about 20 years to degrade. And that's just the lining. The plastic lids? They take even longer to break down, lingering in our environment for centuries.

Think about the disposable cup you use once and toss it away. It could end up in a landfill, on the ocean shores, or clogging drainage systems, contributing to the massive plastic waste problem. If you drank two cups of coffee a day for 20 years, you would have added 10,000 cups to this mounting pile of waste. That's roughly 473 liters of garbage—proof that a small habit can have huge consequences.

Awareness of the problem is the first step. There are easy actions you can take to minimize your impact. A sure winner is to use refillable containers. Many shops are happy to fill your reusable mug; some even offer discounts for doing so.

Alternatively, if you're enjoying your coffee at the shop, opt for a regular cup instead of a disposable one. These small choices might seem trivial, but collectively, they make a substantial difference. By using reusable cups, you're directly contributing in reducing the staggering amounts of plastic waste.

While the convenience of disposable coffee cups is undeniable, the environmental impact is far from negligible. By switching to refillable containers or drinking from a regular cup, you can enjoy your daily brew while being kinder to the planet. Let's all do our part in reducing plastic pollution, one coffee cup at a time.

Cutting Out Soft Drinks

Up until three months ago, I had 55 years of unwavering loyalty to soft drinks. This began in kindergarten when I had to squeeze for space in the bustling school canteen to buy Lemolime+, a brand that, sadly, is now defunct.

When I was a student in Cebu, I paired glazed camote cue (sweet potato) with a local cola brand that recently popularized the trend of packing food home from parties.

My chairperson has always admonished me to avoid artificial sweeteners, regularly forwarding me medical studies highlighting their adverse effects. There was even a time when I had waiters pour my drink into a wine glass, discarding the can. This way, it appeared as though I was savoring red wine—bubbles hidden from view—when in reality, I was drinking a soft drink.

From a habitual three to four cans daily, I deliberately reduced my intake to one can. I sometimes switched brands, opting for the second cola whenever available, enjoying its maximum refreshment. Gradually, I cut my consumption from one can a day to none at all.

Do I still feel a sense of loyalty to those brands? Absolutely. However, I must acknowledge my mortality and the real possibility that sugar and its alternatives are detrimental to my health.

Environmental concerns also play a role in my decision. Plastic pollution remains a major problem, despite soda companies' commitments to reducing landfill waste. While aluminum recycling is relatively efficient, recycling plastic bottles remains a big challenge, with dismal results thus far.

Reflecting on my past consumption, I realize I had too much of a good thing. It was finally time to make a permanent, positive change. Water is it.

Good Buy or Goodbye

There is an outright conflict between environmental issues and business. The environment begs you to be satisfied with less, while stores want you to buy fast fashion. Glossy ads have encouraged consumption.

Now, every time I see something nice in the mall, I ask myself if I really need it. Does it outweigh the fact that resources will be extracted from the planet just to satisfy me? I need to stop the linear economy (extract-produce-use-dump) at the point of purchase. What I am already consuming, I need to consciously reuse, or recycle.

But here lies another conflict—if everyone starts behaving the same way, jobs will be lost.

The solution is for companies to declare and implement their sustainability plan, commit to Circular Economy principles where goods are designed for reuse and recycle, and be ready to be audited. Some brands are already doing this.

We should not shortchange nature, as she can be our biggest ally. Cities globally, even a company in Mindanao, have shown that our biggest problems, like flooding, can be solved naturally or by using solutions that combine with traditional methods. It just needs society to come together, bring interdisciplinary expertise to the table, and build something beautiful and useful.

Banks and companies can consider ecosystem-based adaptation as cost reduction or risk management. We also need to calculate the value of ecosystem assets as, in truth, they reduce damage to communities and property.

This paradox of our world today reminds me of the opening lines from the *Tale of Two Cities* by Charles Dickens (1859): *It was the best of times, it was the worst of times, it was the age of wisdom, it was the age of foolishness.*

If we don't change the way we do business, we may soon find ourselves quoting another of his line "…*we had nothing before us.*"

> "
Doing the right thing is its own reward.

Chapter Fifteen

Do the Right Thing

Ten years ago, I sat in the Harvard Business School auditorium to listen to Professor Rebecca Henderson's lecture on *Reimagining Capitalism*. Her vision included redefining businesses to become engines of positive change, contributing to a more sustainable, equitable, and prosperous world.

Her lecture resonated with my perspective of capitalism, and has gradually influenced my thinking since that day in May 2014. To me, it is simply about enlightened and sustainable giving.

Its Own Reward

There are studies showing that companies with policies benefiting the society and the planet perform better than those that don't make the same effort.

However, other scholarly articles argue there is no such relationship. It's like telling companies not to expect anything in return.

So, what now?

I think it matters that investors are beginning to discriminate between companies that advocate for ESG (Environmental, Social, and Governance) policies and those that don't. Investment bankers even mention that ESG bonds tend to get slightly cheaper funding. The logic makes sense, although it is still unclear whether this is actually happening.

However, the mistake, I believe, is that people and companies expect to be immediately rewarded for their ESG efforts. Or are told that they will reap benefits in the short term.

Digressing a bit, this reminds me of the line *Read today, Lead tomorrow* which I saw weekly in newspapers as a kid. It sounded like a sensible quote, but did anyone really read so they will become leaders in the future? I did not. I just loved reading, very much. I kept reading just for the sheer joy of it.

The greater mistake, I am convinced, is expecting anything in return. It is sufficient to have peace of mind and the satisfaction of knowing you acted according to your values. Altruism has always been part of human nature; it has helped us survive as a species.

One time, after visiting an archaeological site in Penjikent, Tajikistan, our car got stuck in mud that was deceptively covered with snow. Local citizens stopped to help, someone got a shovel, and we were off in 20 minutes. Gestures like this remind me of the goodness of the human race.

Doing the right thing is its own reward.

Academia-Business Partnership—Thriving in the Future

If you believe Hollywood, you might be convinced that the end is near. Why have we chosen to picture a world that is moving toward human extinction?

I choose to view it otherwise. Whether we survive or not depends on whether we believe we will. I have decided to never underestimate human beings. Despite being unable to outsprint predators in the African savannah and being smaller than the mammoth, humans have become the masters of the planet.

All of this happened because of mankind's greatest tool—the one between our ears. Human intelligence invented the wheel, the plow, irrigation, the sailboat, the telescope, and to the misfortune of non-STEM students, algebra and calculus. All these inventions, and many others that followed, provided food security, mobility, and the ability to understand our world and exploit its resources. We also discovered that crude oil could be a source of fuel and, 80 years ago, be turned into a substance called plastic. Oh, what glorious discoveries they were—and the best examples of unintended consequences.

Now, I dare say that human intelligence has grown even more powerful with the advent of artificial intelligence and advanced technology. While we are arguing about AI's role in the future, an emerging consensus suggests that the real benefit does not come from AI replacing humans. The optimal benefit comes from AI augmenting human beings.

Which is why I think Hollywood is mistaken, grossly so. I believe that never in the history of mankind have we found this much intellectual power. We stand on the precipice of a new era. An era where advanced technology, specifically Artificial Intelligence (AI), holds the promise to tackle some of the most pressing challenges of our time. From combating climate change to promoting social equity, AI's transformative potential is immense.

We can think much faster. We can think more deeply. And truly, as what that Apple computer ad claimed many moons ago: we can think differently.

Business cannot do this alone; that would be a mistake. The biggest talent source will continue to be the academia. Let's take a fascinating journey into the future, where advanced technologies reshape the business landscape and academia joins forces with industry to forge a new path forward.

Six years ago, our bank decided to bet on AI and built a 40-person data science team. After developing over 50 machine learning models predicting customer behavior and churning credit scores, we are now moving toward using GenAI to suggest personalized sales pitches to our salespeople, making them more productive. This has been exciting, but let's look at the bigger picture of how AI can help address society's grand challenges.

Let me start with Climate Change. AI can be employed in various solutions to this problem, like renewable energy technology. I am particularly keen on nuclear fusion, as almost 2 years ago, scientists produced a net energy gain from fusion for the first time. Just this year, Princeton engineers used AI controllers to predict plasma instability in fusion reactors milliseconds ahead of time, preventing instability of fusion reactors. I am a physicist by training, and I find this simply awesome.

Meantime, in the area of disaster control—where our country tops the vulnerability list—climate modeling will help policymakers make better informed decisions on mitigation and adaptation measures.

The Philippines is one of the biggest ocean plastic polluters in the world, as multinational companies have been using single-use plastics to distribute their products in what they call our "sachet economy" (Borrelle et al., 2020). I find that term condescending, as it implies that the socio-economic status of our countrymen is to blame. I am partly pacified because there's a new regulation called *Extended Producer Responsibility,* which demands large companies to collect and recycle

100% of the plastic they distribute by 2028. The problem, however, is that only 2% of the 9% plastic collected globally is properly recycled (OECD, 2022). We will need AI-powered recycling systems to identify and separate different types of plastics more accurately than manual sorting. Now, specific to my country, I hope for AI-driven systems that can monitor plastic pollution in our oceans and rivers, providing basis for prompt action to clean up affected areas.

The circular economy is a crucial concept for sustainability. AI can assist in designing products that are easier to recycle and reuse. AI can also provide transparency in supply chains, so that companies can manage the origin and transportation of materials and ensure that circular economy practices are followed. I am also particularly interested in how AI can help facilitate the sharing economy, as it reduces the need for resources.

Social inequality has been the root cause of many upheavals and revolutions through millennia. The proven solution has always been access to quality education—yet, in most countries, this remains a privilege of the upper class. I have already seen AI at work in e-learning platforms like Coursera. In the future, quality education will become more accessible to the underserved communities. The same eLearning sites have been providing competency-based training to upskill people and match them with higher-value jobs.

In financial inclusion, the challenge has been the high cost of credit processing, as most individuals at the base of the pyramid lack credit histories. Fintech start-ups have been experimenting with AI-generated alternative credit scores.

In finance, blockchain will streamline transactions, reduce fraud, and cut out intermediaries. Healthcare will see blockchain securing medical records. Despite still limited applications, this remains in our toolkit as a promising technology for the future. Universities will be breeding grounds for blockchain innovation, hosting hackathons and incubators for the next big blockchain solution.

With Internet of Things or IoT, I am most keen on seeing how it can help feed 10 billion people in the future. It turns out we will be able to do so, if we stop being wasteful in agriculture, food production, and consumption. IoT-led precision agriculture can minimize waste of fertilizer, pesticide, and water, ensuring that crops receive the right inputs at the right time. Together with AI, IoT-driven technologies can monitor crop health, soil conditions, and other parameters, helping farmers in real time.

5G promises lightning-fast connections, boosting IoT, enhancing mobile experiences, and ushering in a new era of AR and VR. Universities will be at the forefront of 5G research, exploring both its potentials and limitations.

With great power comes great responsibility—and a whole lot of cyber threats. As businesses dive deeper into technology, cybersecurity becomes crucial than ever. Companies will need robust security measures, from multi-factor authentication to encryption algorithms. Actually, the need is even more basic—we need cybersecurity professionals. Cybersecurity programs in universities will churn out the next generation of cyber warriors.

How will academia evolve in this tech-driven future? Universities will have to overhaul their curricula, integrate courses on AI, blockchain, IoT, and more. Graduates will enter the job market equipped with in-demand skills, making them highly competitive.

Combining online resources with traditional classroom instruction can offer students with flexibility. This allows us to expand enrollment without needing a proportional increase in physical assets.

Advanced tech will open new frontiers in research. Academia will dive into AI, blockchain, IoT, and 5G, pushing boundaries of what's possible. Universities and research institutions will share knowledge and resources, driving innovation while maintaining a competitive edge.

As technology evolves, ethical considerations will take center stage. Academia will lead the charge in addressing issues like data privacy, algorithmic bias, and the ethical use of AI. Regular dialogues will help ensure that ethical considerations keep pace with technological advancements, preventing potential misuse.

Why is academia crucial here? It's because academic research has been keen on the grand challenges I just mentioned. However, the journals I've read in my DBA class mainly focused on understanding the problem and the need for future research.

Institutions that have married business with AI and other advanced technology, and have experimented with smart cities, are uniquely positioned because we need to move toward actual solutions.

Imagine a world where businesses and academia are inseparable. They'll collaborate on everything from curriculum development to groundbreaking research. Picture this—businesses and universities teaming up to create innovation hubs where students and professionals work side by side. Companies will provide real-world problems, and students will develop innovative solutions.

This partnership between business and academia won't end at graduation. Lifelong learning will become the norm, with professionals returning to university for upskilling and reskilling. Executive education programs will ensure they stay ahead of the curve, always equipped with the latest knowledge and skills.

In this uncertain new world, the partnership between business and academia will be more crucial than ever, with each bringing unique strengths to the table. This partnership will drive progress, ensuring that both sectors thrive in the face of technological change.

With the right business partnerships, we can lead the change for a better world.

Is Doing Good Worth the Trouble?

One weekend, I read a management journal article on Corporate Social Responsibility (CSR) as part of our course materials. It started by reviewing the perennial debate on whether CSR results in any discernible benefit in company value, such as stock prices. From previous readings, I remember more articles arguing there's no relationship than those claiming a positive one.

I do not agree with either position because I believe they both miss the point. If the focus is philanthropy, then there are better measures, starting with the number of activities undertaken (such as trees planted) and extending to the benefits received by the community (such as the number of scholars who graduated). Traditional CSR activities like this are virtually untraceable to share price unless one makes generous assumptions or has a creative imagination to produce some hint of linear regression.

In this type of traditional philanthropic CSR, companies can help the communities around them by providing access to opportunities and resources. For example, my father's company provided quality education to barrio residents, helping thousands of children prepare for university education and scholarships. This is commendable, particularly in a society where social inequality is a primary issue. I personally benefited from this.

There is another approach that complements the old method. Businesses can develop new products and services that address society's grand challenges. I found out that this concept is referred to as Shared Value. I watched a YouTube lecture by renowned strategy professor Michael Porter (2010), who argued that businesses can generate the resources required to solve various issues better than NGOs and governments can. More importantly, they can generate a profit, allowing the solution to be scaled up. Naturally, businesses will choose societal issues where their existing resources, including internal management expertise, are uniquely positioned to address.

For example, a bank might choose to actively support renewable energy projects and deliberately stop funding coal plants. Over time, this has become a source of expertise for them, leading to more project financing transactions.

The same bank has also been a pioneer in digital transformation. Consistent with their founder's vision, they advocate financial inclusion by providing access to formal banking to millions of countrymen living in towns with no bank branches. They built a business that meets a pressing social need while maintaining a competitive edge. And it is scalable.

In a society where problems vastly overwhelm the institutions designed to solve them, I believe business leaders should step up and see if there are challenges they are uniquely equipped to address.

When that happens, they will be true to what business is all about: meeting a need.

Epilogue: Sixty is Nifty

Almost everyone is raw at a younger age. With notable exceptions, we mellow with the years, particularly when aged in nurturing environments—like oloroso sherry casks imparting life's fragrant and flavorful lessons to vintage whiskey.

I like myself better now than when I first became CEO almost 15 years ago, or even when I first joined the bank in 1987. Being raised in the Citi environment—even in the frantic trading rooms—insulated me from the real roughness of the outside world. The high walls defended us when times were tough, with one event in 2008 as the exception. The business card opened doors, but I soon realized that it was the bank I stood for, not myself.

At 45, I ventured outside, believing I was ready for anything. I underestimated human nature, to put it mildly. Planting goodwill was not enough when dealing with people incapable of altruism and empathy. The real world taught me lessons I have long forgiven but never forgotten. One moves on and doesn't keep score, although I have always said that looking good is the best revenge.

Like wine or whiskey, these lessons became part of me. The sweet came with the sour and bitter; I decided I was game for a bit of acidity and peatiness. It all came together. Even the bad made me a better man.

The sweet came with the mentors and senior Citibankers I continue to listen to and who keep in touch; the members of the treasury tribe I see every now and then; and my mentees who have made me proud with their achievements.

One Saturday, my Singapore mentees and colleagues joined me for my book launch. From 3:00 PM to 4:30 PM, I was transported back to 2001 to 2004, when I first met most of them. I count myself lucky.

Now, I am 60, but not complaining. Turning 60 has given me a multitude of benefits I was aware of before but never truly realized the importance of.

Take, for example, airports. As a senior citizen, I get to skip the very, very long immigration queue. This perk makes me feel like a VIP. When paying in a restaurant, the senior discount never fails to make me smile. My only issue is that some establishments prefer to use the term "elderly" on their signs instead of "senior citizen," probably because it is shorter. The icon shows an old man with a cane. I insist, seniors appear younger these days.

Maybe that's just me, refusing to fully accept biology's consequences. But I genuinely believe the term "senior citizen" acknowledges that many of us remain active and spend well into our later years. In hindsight, these benefits have become a collective silver lining to the passage of time, matching well with my fast-thinning salt and pepper.

However, the obligation to share my time with those seeking guidance or for those with dilemmas to discuss, does not stop. The more of me I give, whether virtually or through my books, the more of me remains to be shared—the good, the bad, and the not-so-pretty.

Whatever comes after, I no longer feel the need to keep score. I have already beaten my younger self. And that, to me, is more than enough. Through all these years of reinventing and outperforming myself, with family and friends by my side, I never stood alone.

Acknowledgments

I want to express my gratitude to Hong Koon Chua, publishing director at World Scientific, for his invaluable guidance on how to position, outline, and market this book.

Thank you to my professors, Daniel Broby, Babak Hayati, Gerry Santa Maria, Raul Rodriguez, Felipe Calderon, Jammu Francisco, and Corinne Burgos, for enriching my views, challenging me to study harder, and deepening my insights.

I am also indebted to my colleagues—Pam Cabudoy, Jahzeel Sartillo-Buenaventura, Thea Dizon, and Rafael Triguero—for carefully reviewing my early posts and manuscripts and suggesting edits to better convey my message.

And finally, to my secretary, Irene Yangzon, for helping me with many important things—far too many to list. Thank you.

References

Ambrose, S. E. (1992). *Band of Brothers: E Company, 506th Regiment, 101st Airborne from Normandy to Hitler's Eagle's Nest*. Simon & Schuster.

Borrelle, S. B., Ringma, J., Lavender Law, K., Monnahan, C. C., Lebreton, L., McGivern, A., Murphy, E., Jambeck, J., Leonard, G. H., Hilleary, M. A., Eriksen, M., Possingham, H. P., De Frond, H., Gerber, L. R., Polidoro, B., Tahir, A., Bernard, M., Mallos, N., Barnes, M. and Rochman, C. M. (2020). Predicted growth in plastic waste exceeds efforts to mitigate plastic pollution. *Science*, 369(6509), 1515-1518. https://doi.org/10.1126/SCIENCE.ABA3656

Burns, R. (1788). Auld lang syne [Song]. On Traditional Songs. Various Labels.

Cataldi, E. F., Bennett, C. T. and Chen, X. (2018). First-generation students: College access, persistence, and postbachelor's outcomes (NCES 2018-421). National Center for Education Statistics. https://nces.ed.gov/pubsearch/pubsinfo.asp?pubid=2018421

CECP. (2010, August 10). *Michael Porter: Creating Shared Value* [Video]. YouTube. https://www.youtube.com/watch?v=z2oS3zk8VA4

Clooney, G. (Director). (2023). *The Boys in the Boat* [Film]. Amazon MGM Studios.

Desir, R., Rakestraw, J., Seavey, S., Wainberg, J. and Young, G. (2023). Managerial ability, CEO age and the moderating effect of firm characteristics. *Journal of Business Finance & Accounting*, 51(1-2), 148–179. https://doi.org/10.1111/jbfa.12689

Dickens, C. (1859). *A tale of two cities*. Chapman & Hall.

Ferreira, T. M. S., Ramos, S. and Marques, C. S. (2017). Motivational factors in sales team management and their influence on individual performance. *Journal of Business & Industrial Marketing*, 32(6), 838-848. https://doi.org/10.1108/JBIM-06-2016-0133

Kibria, M. G., Masuk, N. I., Safayet, R., Nguyen, H. Q., and Mourshed, M., (2023). Plastic waste: Challenges and opportunities to mitigate pollution and effective management. *International Journal of Environmental Research*, 17(1). https://doi.org/10.1007/s41742-023-00507-z

Mercury, F. (1978). Don't Stop Me Now [Song]. On Jazz. EMI.

Mills, C. M., Goldstein, T. R., Kanumuru, R. K., Monroe, A. J. and Quintero, M. (2024). Debunking the Santa myth: The process and aftermath of becoming skeptical about Santa. *Developmental Psychology*, 60(3), 412–427. https://doi.org/10.1037/dev0001729

Murakami, H. (2008). *What I Talk About When I Talk About Running*. Alfred A. Knopf.

National Oceanic and Atmospheric Administration [NOAA]. (2021). How long until it's gone? Marine Debris Program. https://marinedebris.noaa.gov/discover-marine-debris/how-long-until-its-gone

Olenski, A. R., Abola, M. V., and Jena, A. B. (2015). Do heads of government age more quickly? Observational study comparing mortality between elected leaders and runners-up in national elections of 17 countries. *BMJ*. https://doi.org/10.1136/bmj.h6424

Organisation for Economic Co-operation and Development (OECD). (2022). *Global Plastics Outlook: Economic Drivers, Environmental Impacts and Policy Options*. OECD Publishing, Paris. https://doi.org/10.1787/de747aef-en

Pew Research Center (2021, May 18). First-generation college graduates lag behind their peers on key economic outcomes. https://www.pewresearch.org/social-trends/2021/05/18/first-generation-college-graduates-lag-behind-their-peers-on-key-economic-outcomes/

Rackham, N. (1988). *SPIN Selling*. McGraw-Hill.

Rosé and Mars, B. (2024). APT [Song]. On Rosie. Atlantic Records.

Schweiger, S., Stouten, H., and Bleijenbergh, I. L. (2018). A system dynamics model of resistance to organizational change: The role of participatory strategies, *Systems Research and Behavioral Science*, 35(6), 658-674. https://doi.org/10.1002/sres.2509

Shakespeare, W. (1601). *Twelfth Night* [Play].

Shakespeare, W. (1599). *Julius Caesar* [Play].

Sherman, R. B. and Sherman, R. M. (1964). It's a small world (after all) [Song]. On It's a Small World. Disneyland Records.

Sinek, S. (2020, June 25). *What Makes the Highest Performing Teams in the World* [Video]. YouTube. https://www.youtube.com/watch?v=zP9jpxitfb4

Spice Girls. (2007). *Headlines (Friendship Never Ends)* [Song]. On *Greatest Hits*. Virgin Records.

Toubson, A. (2024, February 15). Company loses $25 million to deepfake scam. *TechGriot*. Retrieved from https://techgriot.co/english/news/2024/02/company-loses-25-million-to-deepfake-scam/

Underwood, F. (2013). *House of Cards* [Television series]. Netflix.

Vohs, K. D., Redden, J. P. and Rahinel, R. (2013). Physical order produces healthy choices, generosity, and conventionality, whereas disorder produces creativity. *Psychological Science*, 24(9), 1860-1867. https://doi.org/10.1177/0956797613480186

Wasserman, N. (2008). The founder's dilemma. *Harvard Business Review*, 86(2), 102-109. https://hbr.org/2008/02/the-founders-dilemma

Index